From Losers
to Winners

To CHRISTINE

From Losers to Winners

BREAKTHROUGH AT BRYANT HIGH

ENJOY!!

Marvin Findling

For confidentiality purposes and to protect the privacy of certain individuals, many names, places and identifying details have been changed.

Copyright © 2015 Marvin Findling
All rights reserved.
ISBN: 1508848785
ISBN 13: 9781508848783
Library of Congress Control Number: 2015904159
CreateSpace Independent Publishing Platform
North Charleston, South Carolina

To Christine,

Dedication

To my wife, Anne, whose inspiration and patience contributed to the completion of my book

And to my former students:
I want to let you know that your learning experiences also enriched my life. It was my good fortune and honor to be associated with every one of you. What a plethora of memories. God bless you all.

Your teacher and friend,
Marvin Findling
marvfind@optonline.net

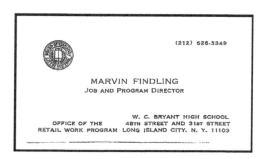

(212) 626-3349

MARVIN FINDLING
JOB AND PROGRAM DIRECTOR

W. C. BRYANT HIGH SCHOOL
OFFICE OF THE   48TH STREET AND 31ST STREET
RETAIL WORK PROGRAM LONG ISLAND CITY, N. Y. 11103

Table of Contents

Acknowledgments

✳✳✳

I wish to express my sincere appreciation to the Morningside Writers Group for their helpful critiques and encouragement. The group was very motivating and gave me the confidence to continue writing.

Special thanks to Gene Hull, moderator of the group, whose comments—whether positive or negative—were so well appreciated. They contributed to my growth as a writer and the desire to complete my book.

Additional thanks to Larry Guess and everyone else for their editing by committee. What a pleasure to be associated with such a wonderful group

Also, to my good friends, Rosie of the Fountains, Mary Ellen, Mike Sample, and especially Anna L.

Introduction

✳✳✳

Many of the stories in this book involve students who formed the foundation of the Retail Work Program. At the time, they may have been considered disruptive, undisciplined, incorrigible, or whatever the terminology was. Perhaps they qualified for all of the aforementioned characteristics.

Every chapter in the book refers to events, true experiences, some humorous, some sad, mostly occurring while the program was still in its infancy. Only the names have been changed.

But life changes, and these same students formed the background for what eventually became a standout program that was recognized and honored by many businesses, city councilmen, the school principal, the Board of Education of the City of New York, and most important, the students themselves (*see* testimonials).

Without boring you, the reader, with statistics of how many eventually entered the legal field, the medical field, or the world of finance, the following statistic is the most relevant and makes me proudest of all: 90 percent of the students who at one time or another were involved in the Retail Work Program subsequently attended college.

Mentioned in chapter 1 as the leader of the losers, I truly ended up as the leader of the winners. It was an honor to participate in the transition.

Enjoy!

Mini-School – The Beginning

***

Once upon a time, circa 1975, the administration at W. C. Bryant High School in Queens initiated a specialized program designed for students who had been previously expelled for a variety of reasons, from disciplinary action to almost incorrigible behavior. Hopefully, as a last resort, this program would be successful in keeping them in the educational system.

Students would be allowed amnesty, provided they were willing to participate in the program, called mini-school. They would be taught by a group of six teachers, including me. Our selection was based on teaching skills, rapport with students, and ability to maintain class control. We were humorously classified by some members of the faculty as the "leaders of the losers."

Math, English, history, science, and languages, plus an assortment of electives, composed the curriculum. If students found certain subjects more interesting than others, they had the option of attending that subject class more than once a day, provided it was in accordance with an intended maximum attendance requirement of twenty-four students per class.

I was selected to teach certain subjects that would relate to meaningful life experiences, among which were business and criminal law. The latter subject was popular to the point where, on many occasions, students would remain in class for two or three consecutive periods. This often resulted in an attendance of fifty or more students in the classroom, well above the intended maximum. A number of them sat on the floor, completely attentive and with minimal discipline problems.

We had many guest speakers, including police officers and a defense attorney, who spoke on topics such as petty larceny, grand larceny, search procedures, statutory rape, etc., any of which some of the students may have had personal experience.

Actually, one of the mini-school students, Arthur Chandler, was at the time being represented pro bono by the defense attorney. Arthur had been arrested on an assault charge relating to an altercation that had occurred near school grounds.

About five of the twenty-five students from the criminal law class, attending the hearing at the Queens courthouse, were called as witnesses. Each one would innocently do the Michael Jackson moonwalk when approaching the stand and individually testify that Arthur, having been physically assaulted, was simply defending himself.

When the judge realized that the defense attorney intended to call the remaining twenty students to the stand, he complimented their loyalty and dismissed the case, but not before requesting and hearing Arthur's rendition of Frankie Lyman's "Why Do Fools Fall in Love," which the judge had heard during an earlier recess.

Two weeks later, Arthur suffered a severe concussion while playing basketball in a church gymnasium and passed away. All the students and teachers from the mini-school attended the funeral services.

Beginning with their court appearance and the 100 percent funeral attendance, it became apparent that a bond was being forged between the students and the teachers of the mini-school. Perhaps they weren't such a bunch of losers after all, which was eventually proven to be the case.

Read on.

CHAPTER 2

Fringe Benefits

✳✳✳

There were many positive ventures that were developed as features of the mini-school, subsequently called the Retail Work Program or RWP, of which I became the director.

As a reward for improved attendance, punctuality, grades, peer-teacher relationships, and general improvement in work-related skills, many students of the Retail Work Program were offered part-time after-school positions in local businesses. These included retail clothing, food stores, and a local bank. Other students were offered jobs that involved traveling into Manhattan. This presented the opportunities for employment at retail stores such as Bloomingdale's and Alexander's; Wall Street firms, including Merrill Lynch and Bache & Co.; and First National City Bank.

Besides receiving excellent salaries, students were graded by their employers for job performance. The grades became part of their school records. All of the firms were very receptive to students from our program. Many students remained with their employers while attending college, and some were retained full time and eventually promoted to managerial positions.

In addition to the financial rewards, these jobs had a tremendous influence on the students social outlook (maturity level).

Aside from their relationship with parents, friends, and teachers, they had a better understanding of the people they were associated with in the business world.

Included in the above were employment situations that created negative as well as positive experiences, contributing toward making the students more worldly wise.

The following was an example.

CHAPTER 3

Honesty Prevails

✳✳✳

In early November, I received a phone call from Mr. Rick Richards, an assistant store manager at C-Town, a local food store we were doing business with. He proceeded to comment on the two students he had recently hired as part-time cashiers. He said, "In addition to the two students we recently hired, we now have a total of four students from your Retail Work Program employed as cashiers at C-Town, and we are very pleased with their work effort. The purpose of my call is to thank you."

What a great call, and so rewarding! It made my day.

About one month later, on a Monday morning, I was informed by three of the four students that Mr. Richards was constantly finding shortages when he compared their register cash with the register readings at the end of the day. He actually accused each of the students of pocketing some of the money, which he stated was the reason for the shortages. As a result, he would once again be deducting the shortage amounts from their earnings at the end of the week.

Together and individually, the students told me that they were very diligent in performing their work duties, especially after they experienced the deductions from their prior week's earnings. In fact, they felt that the Mr. Richards was responsible for the shortages, pocketing the differences for which they were charged. Their new nickname for him was "Slick Rick."

One of the students, Anita Hollins, said, "Practically every time I look in his direction, I see or hear Slick Rick on the phone. He sounds just like my uncle Richie, who is constantly on the phone with someone named Ace, always talking about horses."

Twice that morning I called Robert Bickford, the store manager. I left messages but didn't receive a callback. I then instructed the students not to report to work that afternoon.

The following morning Mr. Bickford called, informing me of the bedlam at the store the previous day due to the shortage of cashiers. After I told him that I had called him twice the prior day and left unanswered messages, I explained the reason for my calls and the students' absences.

I also informed him that the deductions were actually causing the students to earn less than minimum wage, and I was about to send them for job interviews at McDonald's, which had four positions available at a higher hourly wage and with a more trusting employer/employee relationship.

Within one hour, Mr. Bickford called me back and said, "Thanks for making me aware of the situation. I'm informing you that after careful investigation, Mr. Richards has been terminated, and all deducted earnings will be refunded, including lost wages from the prior day. Also, in appreciation of their satisfactory job performance, each student will receive a fifteen-cent hourly increase in pay, except for Anita Hollins, who will receive a twenty-five-cent hourly increase in her new role as temporary assistant manager.

Hopefully, all of the above should remedy the situation, and I look forward to their return this afternoon."

I complied with his request. Thus ended the one-day "strike".

Following her graduation that year, Anita Hollins was promoted to Slick Rick Richards former position—permanent assistant store manager.

✳✳✳

Anita attended Baruch College at night, receiving a BA degree in marketing and management.

Subsequently, she became a store manager for Associated Food Stores, followed by a supervisory position with the A&P food chain.

CHAPTER 4

George's Ghostly Return

✳✳✳

George Pappas wasn't excited about attending his European history class, especially since he was not an enthusiast of the subject matter.

What he felt was more educational was the subject matter he encountered while attending one of the Retail Work Program courses: criminal law. Guest speakers, such as defense attorneys and law enforcement officers, positively contributed to the learning experience. Actually, George's interest in attending the class was twofold. If the subject matter got a little boring, he could always entertain himself by observing the length of the miniskirts worn by the female students.

In order to avoid attending the aforementioned history class, George, without my knowledge, had one of his peers inform the teacher, Ms. Jefferies, during the first week of the semester, that he had met his unfortunate demise and therefore would no longer attend her class. Meanwhile, George continued to attend my criminal law class during what he claimed to be his daily study period and was an important contributor to classroom discussion.

It is worth mentioning that at the time, George was stout to the point where it was not easy for him to fit into or remove himself from his desk, which was located near the rear door of the classroom.

One morning, Ms. Jefferies, the history teacher, came into my classroom and walked up to my desk. Shaking, she looked white as a ghost. "While walking along the hallway," she said, "I peered in the window of the rear door of your classroom and saw the ghost of George Pappas, my deceased student, staring at me. Also, the ghost was in Technicolor."

We both looked in the direction of the window, but there was no George and no desk. I said, "Ms. Jefferies, watch my class while I investigate."

I opened the classroom door and looked outside. There was George, waddling along and then disappearing around a hallway corner, still stuck to his desk. Within ten seconds, Ms. Jefferies appeared next to me.

We peered down the hallway and saw nothing. Her vision of George had disappeared, and so did Ms. Jefferies, muttering something about taking a medical sabbatical.

My adventures with George did not end as his teacher. Following my retirement from the educational field, I sold life insurance, and somewhere along the way, a slimmed down George became one of my clients, as did many of his relatives.

Unfortunately, one of my clients died accidentally, and at the wake I met George and some of the above-mentioned relatives. George informed me that a number of his friends were at the wake, and he asked me for some business cards that he could pass on to them.

Considering our current surroundings, a funeral parlor, and since George was now a happily married man with two children, I assumed his days as a practical joker was over. I expressed my appreciation for his efforts on my behalf and handed him six business cards.

Within the next half hour, some of the deceased's relatives approached and lectured me about my thoughtlessness and lack of respect. Now feeling very uncomfortable, I decided to leave.

I again approached the casket in order to pay my last respects. There, embedded between two fingers of the corpse, whose arms were folded across each other, were my business cards, with the top one clearly printed, TAKE ONE.

CHAPTER 5

Pal's Pals

***

Because a family problem, requiring my wife to be out of town for a week, conflicted with my job schedule, I had difficulty locating doggie care for my collie, Pal.

My only alternative was to keep Pal with me as much as possible. This included occasionally bringing him to school, which proved difficult at times. When entering the building, I would avoid security, and then hide Pal in the students' well-ventilated wardrobe closet.

Students attending my classes were fully aware of the situation and made every effort to keep it a secret. This was not easy, considering the number of times Pal had to be carried out of the building to be relieved and then returned by my loyal students, 90 percent of whom were African American. They kept insisting that Pal must belong to the Ku Klux Klan because he kept barking only at the African American pedestrians on the street. They also thought he could possibly be a transvestite, because he straddled like a female instead of urinating in the usual male position.

One day, the chairman of the department, Mr. McGee, walked into my classroom, claiming he heard a dog barking. Immediately, some of the students started barking. Mr. McGee commented on the sanity of the students and walked out. He returned to the class-room ten minutes later, again claiming that he heard a dog bark-ing. Once again, students started barking, at which point Calvin Williams, sitting at a desk in front of mine, retrieved a can of dog food, an opener, and the spoon that was lying on my desk. Mr. McGee noticed this and with a triumphant "Aha!" questioned what Calvin was doing with a can of dog food. Calvin responded by opening the can. He scooped a spoonful, proceeded to eat it, and then offered a spoonful to Mr. McGee, who refused, looking pale as a ghost. He once again commented on the mental condition of the students and *ran* out of the room.

Mr. McGee religiously avoided the classroom, which he clas-sified as the "cuckoo's nest," until he observed, while zooming past the room one day, that every student was reading a newspa-per, namely the *New York Times*. He burst into the room, demand-ing to know why students were wasting educational time reading newspapers.

I informed him that the students were actually involved in a serious learning experience, the study of the stock market, which was an important part of the consumer education curriculum. They were reviewing the financial section of the *Times* and analyz-ing the performance of a stock that they had invested in earlier that month, at a cost of five dollars per student, or whatever they could afford.

Mr. McGee then questioned the feasibility of students study-ing the stock market, considering their economic status. Calvin Williams, the dog food gourmet from the prior day, asked Mr. McGee to name a stock that was in his current portfolio. When he heard the name, Calvin, our self-appointed senior research analyst, immediately referred to the stock listing and was able to inform

Mr. McGee of the fifty-two-week high and low, current price, P/E ratio, and dividend yield of the stock. Calvin offered his opinion that he considered the stock to be a dog. At this point he started to bark, which was followed by barks from other students in the classroom, once again reminding Mr. McGee that he had entered the domain of the dog pound.

Calvin then informed Mr. McGee that our stock was up 20 percent since its original purchase date. Upon hearing Mr. McGee's forced compliment, Calvin remarked, "It's amazing what a dog food diet will do for a person's brainpower."

Incidentally, Pal had cut class that day.

CHAPTER 6

False Promises

✳✳✳

Henry Taylor, a senior student in the Retail Work Program, was doing very poorly in his business-law class. His classroom participation, test marks, attendance, homework assignments, and in particular, his indifference to a final project were at a failing level. He disregarded my comments regarding his lack of effort toward improving his situation. My warnings that he would fail the course if he did not improve his work ethic were falling on deaf ears.

I finally called his mother, and the following conversation ensued. "Hello, Mrs. Taylor. I'm Marvin Findling, a teacher at Bryant High School, and I'm calling regarding a problem I'm having with your son, Henry."

Mrs. Taylor replied, "Oh, Mr. Findling. You're the teacher Hank likes and is always talking about."

I replied, "Well, he won't like me so much if he fails my course, especially with him being a senior. That's why I would like to make an appointment with you. We need to discuss the situation further—and the sooner, the better—because his final grade has to be submitted following his final exam."

Mrs. Taylor said, "I'm sorry, but I'm in the middle of Botox and cellulite treatments, and I have continuous appointments the next few weeks. Cancellation of any of these appointments can negatively affect the treatments. By the way, my name is Barbara, but you can call me Bobbie. Can I call you Marvin?"

I said, "Henry has to pass his final exam next week, or he will fail the course, which could negatively affect his graduation. Mrs. Taylor, I mean Bobbie, **which negative** is more important?"

She replied, "Would a nice man like you fail my son and ruin his future?"

I said, "Bobbie, you sound just as capable. Why don't you come to my office at three o'clock today, and we can speak to Henry together. I'll retain him after class."

To quote Bobbie, "You're ruining my day, but I'll be there."

Three o'clock came. I was there. Henry was there, but no Barbara (Bobbie). Henry informed me the next day that due to a cancellation, Mrs. Taylor's beautician was able to fit her in at three o'clock for a permanent, and this was the reason for her non-appearance. However, she supplied Henry with a note informing me that she would call within the next few days to set up another appointment.

Such was not the case—no call, no Bobbie.

Although he narrowly passed the final exam, I advised Henry that he was still close to failing the course due to the reasons mentioned above, including his failure to turn in the final project.

The following week, who should appear at my office with Henry but Mrs. Taylor, looking like she had just completed a photo session for the cover of *Vogue Magazine.* She commenced to rant and rave. Her final comment: "You are ruining my son's life!"

My response: "Mrs. Taylor, you are getting so upset that some of the curls from your recent perm are falling out of place."

Henry also had a comment. "Mr. Findling, my plan for the future is to own a funeral parlor, and when I do, the first person I want to embalm is you. And at no additional charge, I'll enclose my completed project in your casket."

Suddenly, Henry turned to his mother, and with tears in his eyes said, "You should have come to see Mr. Findling that afternoon like you promised, but you were more concerned about your good looks than my future. He kept his promise, but you didn't keep yours. I deserve to fail the course, and it might keep me from graduating. But what is more important is that you are failing your responsibilities as my mom."

He then looked directly at me and said, "I apologize for my comment, Mr. Findling, because I know you meant the best, and I let you and myself down."

After successfully passing an additional exam and meeting a revised deadline for a more difficult project, Henry passed the course and graduated on time.

❋❋❋

Henry did go into the funeral business and eventually opened his own funeral parlor. About two years after Henry graduated, Mrs. Taylor (Bobbie) opened a beauty spa in Brooklyn, and called it Marvie de Paris in my honor.

CHAPTER 7

An Example of True Love – Part One

✳✳✳

There were times during the early days of the mini-school when incorrigible behavior traits would return. Fortunately, they were fewer and far between. The following is an example.

Health education was a required course in the curriculum. While temporarily substituting for an absent teacher, I had forewarned the class that the following day there would be a discussion about safe sexual practices, featuring a female guest speaker. Therefore, it came as no surprise to me that on the scheduled day, the entire class plus "friends of students," arrived for the featured event.

But not the guest speaker. I was left on my own.

Topics for discussion included abstinence, the birth control pill, safe sex (condoms), and general hygiene. Halfway through the lesson, I felt most of the class, disappointed and in a complete state of boredom, would start booing me, just to stay awake.

Vermel Ross, a student in the class, raised her hand. When I recognized her, she enthusiastically announced, "Mr. Findling, there are still some of us who employ continued abstinence, who believe in the sanctity of marriage. We are making every effort to preserve our virginity until our wedding night, myself included."

I was thrilled with Vermel's efforts at perfecting and declaring the above statement.

At this point, Tyrone Hill raised his hand and requested permission to respond to Vermel's remarks, which was granted.

Tyrone said, "Vermel, you lie. You've had sex with me and other students in this class."

Vermel replied, "Mr. Findling, don't believe Tyrone. He is not telling the truth. I'm a virgin."

Said Tyrone, "Girl, you are no virgin."

He then turned to another student, Hawthorne Jones, and said, "Hawthorne, you've had sex with Vermel. You told me."

All students' eyes turned in the direction of Hawthorne, who said, "Speak for yourself, Tyrone. I told you shit."

At that point another student, Alicia Williams, asked to speak. "Tyrone, you are a slimeball. Whoever agrees, raise your hand."

A majority of students, male and female, raised their hands, while others voiced their comments vocally, with words like "shithead" and a variety of "fuckin's," such as "fuckin' scumbag."

It was around this time that the guest speaker entered the room, took a look at the class, heard a goodly portion of the conversation, spun around, and made a beeline down the hall, never to be seen again.

The period ended. Vermel left the room with tears in her eyes.

CHAPTER 8

An Example of True Love – Part Two

✳✳✳

That night, I had difficulty falling asleep. I kept thinking that Tyrone was the perfect example of the previously expelled incorrigible outcasts who I was now involved with, when two months earlier, I was happily teaching an American History honors class.

And now here I was, the director, the one who was supposed to make successes of these misfits. *But remember, Marvin, these are children, and you volunteered for this.*

The following day, hearing that the teacher was still absent, I again volunteered to substitute teach her health education class.

I couldn't wait for class to begin.

I immediately passed out blank paper, and was hit with a barrage of "What the f--k is this?"

I said, "At least 80 percent of you are in my regular criminal law class and know my rules, so here is the deal."

I spelled the word F-U-C-K on the blackboard and said, "When I say **GO**, you can write, whisper, yell, scream that word or whatever fits your fancy until I yell **STOP,** at which point you can no longer use it in any classes associated with the Retail Work Program. Violation of this rule will lead to being expelled from the program."

I approached the blackboard and said, "Are there any questions as to how"—I stopped, added an I-N-G to the four-letter word, and continued—"serious I am?"

"**GO**!"

Silence reigned.

"**STOP**!"

I erased the blackboard.

"Now, let's proceed to the matter at hand. I want everyone to write the name of a close friend, sister, or relative whose age is similar to Vermel's."

After waiting a few minutes, I asked, "Would you want that person insulted as Vermel was yesterday by Tyrone, when all she was doing was expressing her moral feelings? And that definitely includes you, Tyrone. Do you have a sister Vermel's age? A cousin Vermel's age? Even if you actually had a relationship with Vermel, would it be necessary to advertise it, to boast about it? You both— or at least, Vermel—deserve the proper respect for something so personal. If anyone disagrees or has an opinion, let's discuss it right here, right now."

Alicia Williams raised her hand, looked directly at him, and emphatically stated, "Tyrone, you are a real shit. Sorry, Mr. Findling."

I said, "Tyrone, you can write a letter of apology. Or better yet, you can be a man, walk right up to Vermel now, and apologize. She is sitting there, right now, in front of you and the class, crying over what you did to her yesterday, and other students are crying with her."

After a period of complete classroom silence, Tyrone walked to Vermel's desk, and in a voice ringing with emotion he said, "Vermel, I wronged you yesterday, and I'm sorry for what I did."

Vermel stood up and said, "Tyrone, no matter how much my moral feelings have frustrated you, and caused our breakup last week, I have to stick to my principles. I still love you, and I always will. Be proud of me."

With that, she got up, and they embraced and kissed, right there in front of the class. Many students applauded, tears also flowing.

What a difference between two days.

To give up an honors class for this? *Anytime.*

CHAPTER 9

A One-Track Mind

✳✳✳

I was sitting at my office desk, awaiting the arrival of his parents to discuss the scholastic progress, or lack thereof, of their son, Donald.

Donald's sole interest was reviewing the sports section of the *Daily News* and handicapping the racing program at Aqueduct Racetrack. He would inform me of his selections at the beginning or end of the period. This was contrary to the subject matter at hand, personal finance, an important chapter in our curriculum on consumer education.

Apparently Donald believed that his handicapping system (and the resulting profits) would greatly contribute to his personal finances, and therefore, it was definitely related to the subject matter. Donald said, "In fact, if you ever take advantage of my expertise and make a few wagers of your own, any profits you derive should be considered in determining my final grade."

I replied, "Donald, although I appreciate your offer to increase my personal wealth, your lack of effort in assignments and classroom activities could eventually lead to failing the course, which is my reason for summoning your parents."

Both of his parents arrived at my office at the scheduled time. Donald's mother was completely dressed in black, giving the impression she was preparing to start mourning after hearing my report regarding her son's miniscule scholastic achievements. His father, Dan, was dressed like he had just posed for the cover of *Gentlemen's Quarterly*. I couldn't resist complimenting his attire, whereupon he informed me that his suit was Armani, and his shoes were by Bruno Magli, from Italy. He noticed me staring at his wife, whose matronly appearance was in sharp contrast to dapper Dan.

Dan said, "We are still in mourning for our daughter, Margarita, who passed away three years ago as a result of an automobile accident. In fact, my wife lights at least ten candles every night in her memory."

I extended my condolences for their loss. We discussed Donald's lack of effort in the class subject matter, and his major interest in an equestrian sport, namely horse racing.

Dan then informed me that he was the owner of a stable of horses that were racing at various tracks around the country. This included pacers and trotters currently racing locally at Yonkers Raceway. We agreed that his business was the obvious reason for Donald's interest.

Dan said, "I assure you that I will discuss this school matter further with Donald, but not this weekend, because Donald has to be driven up to Vernon Downs to collect the winner's check for my trotter, Grand R. Volo, who won the eighth race there last night. Actually, since my son speaks very highly of you as his favorite teacher, I was wondering if you could to do me a big favor. Would you be willing drive Donald up there to collect the check? In fact, I have two horses entered tomorrow at Vernon, in the second and fifth race, and if you get there early enough, you might do very well wagering on my pacer, Speedy Hanover, who I dropped in class in the fifth race and has a shot to win at great odds. Meanwhile, I have to leave now because I have to be at Yonkers to meet the trainer and driver for two of my horses that will be running this evening, one of which is Lincoln Road, who looks good from the second position. And if you happen to come to Yonkers Raceway, look me up because I have my own box."

Following my rejection of his offer, Dan shook my hand and left, followed by his wife, who had been in tears throughout the entire meeting.

Two weeks later, while spending an evening out with a few friends at Yonkers Raceway, who should we run into but Dan, in another *Gentlemen's Quarterly* outfit, accompanied by "my friend Marie," a possible previous or potential candidate for *Penthouse* magazine.

Following my introduction to his lady friend, Dan said, "If you had driven Donald to Vernon Downs, you might have wagered on my horse, Speedy Hanover, who won the fifth race at odds of fifteen to one, but not to worry, because Lincoln Road is entered in the upcoming race at eight to one and is a shoo-in."

I said, "Thanks for your tip. Appreciated. And I'm glad to see you again, but for a more important reason. Your son, Donald, is still failing my course."

Dan replied, "Oops, I forgot to speak to him."

"By the way, how is your wife?" I asked.

"Oh, she's still at home in mourning."

Based on my subsequent discussions with other teachers, it appeared that his father's business and social ventures, plus Donald's sad home life, contributed to his lack of interest in scholastic activities and his failure to graduate on time.

However, Donald achieved success as a handicapper and sports reporter for a local newspaper.

CHAPTER 10

Jill, the Model

✳✳✳

On a Monday morning, I was sitting in my office during a free period, having just completed a phone call to Harold Johnson, the proprietor of a local McDonald's.

I informed him that the weekly hours of employment for the ten students he hired through our Retail Work Program was exceeding the number of hours we had originally agreed upon. My concern was that this excessive work schedule could have a negative effect on the students' schoolwork, and it had to be reduced to conform with our agreement. As a positive ending to our conversation, Mr. Johnson agreed to employ two more students in order to reduce the individual workload.

Within minutes of our conversation, Mr. Johnson called back, stating he was concerned with the behavior of one of my students, Jill O'Toole, one of his favorite employees during the past year. In fact, on several occasions, she had been the recipient of the "employee of the month" bonus award. For the past two weeks, however, contrary to her normal happy behavior, she called in sick, was repeatedly late, and on one occasion, broke out in tears, and had to be sent home. He now felt that what he originally thought was an employment issue was of a more serious nature.

I thanked Mr. Johnson for his concern and told him I would immediately look into the matter.

There was a knock on the door, and Jill walked in. Jill was just about the prettiest girl in our school. She had the stature of a model, was looking forward to a career in modeling, and was paying for a professional portfolio from her earnings at McDonald's. On a previous visit to my office, she had stated, "I desperately want to get out of my house, even if I have to leave school, and get started in a modeling career as soon as possible."

Recently, her grades had fallen noticeably. She now appeared extremely depressed. I was anxious to know why. Sobbing, she told me her sad story, and I will quote her as best I can.

"I am the only child in a household where my father, when drunk, abuses me verbally and physically. Lately, he has been drinking more than ever. Finally, unable to take it any longer, I moved in with my boyfriend. When I returned home to get some of my clothes, my father, again drunk, hit me badly, leaving marks. I was too ashamed to be seen at school or work. Last week, I saw an ad for models in the *Daily News*. I appeared with my portfolio at the advertised address, which was in the Times Square area. I was directed by Lou, the muscle-bound security officer, to room 300, where I met Steve, the person who had placed the ad."

She continued, "Steve examined and complimented my photos. He then told me that he was interested in models of a certain nature, and if hired, I could be earning a minimum of $250 a week. He then informed me that subject to my approval, he would have to take his own pictures of me in a topless state, wearing only a bikini bottom. He wanted to be sure I wouldn't be embarrassed should there be occasions when I would be involved in this type of modeling. Thinking of the earnings possibility, and the independence it would give me, I agreed.

"As he was taking the pictures, Steve remarked how I seemed to be enjoying the posing to the point where I was obviously getting excited down below, and if I allowed him to remove my panties and feel my private part, my future would be guaranteed, and to prove it, he would give me $200 in advance. I seductively approached him, kicked him in his nuts, grabbed my clothes, my portfolio, his camera, and ran out of his office.

"I yelled back at him, 'Don't follow me because I am only sixteen. Go home and play with your wife's dry pussy, if you can find it'.

I got dressed in the stairwell, miraculously removed the film, and gave the camera to Lou, the security officer on the ground floor. I told him that Steve, in room 300 had said, 'Lou is a closet fag. Tell him that as soon as he returns the camera to me, I will personally reward him with a blow job, and an additional $200 if it can be filmed.' Within seconds, there was Lou, bounding upstairs with a bat in his hand, screaming, 'Steve, I'm going to break your fucking legs.'

"On the subway ride home, I cried, but then I laughed at my immediate modeling success, and I went to work at McDonald's that evening in a better frame of mind.

"This morning, I saw my father outside the school. He told me that, having heard that you're my favorite teacher, he wants to talk to you. He doesn't know about my modeling experience, so please don't tell him. He also thinks you know where my boyfriend lives."

I sent Jill back to class, promising her she would have less cause for concern after I spoke to her father.

Within ten minutes, I received a call from the principal's office, stating an upset parent had appeared and requested permission to speak to both Mr. Wilson, the principal, and me. Hearing the name of the parent, James O'Toole, and unsure of his current condition, I mentioned the possible need for security.

In the principal's office, I was immediately confronted by Mr. O'Toole, who said, "How would you feel if your daughter left home, especially an Irish household, and moved in with a nigger? Well, you're her favorite teacher, and she listens to you, so you have to tell her to come home. But then again, maybe you're one of them liberal Jew teachers who don't give a shit whether their children live with or marry niggers and is supporting her decision."

I asked Mr. O'Toole, "Is there any reason for Jill to leave home, including possible physical abuse, considering the fact that she has appeared in class a few times with bruises on her body?"

"You see what I mean?" he said. "That's none of your fuckin' business, and maybe I should kick your ass a couple of times, too."

Now, this conversation was becoming very upsetting to Mr. Wilson, because Mr. O'Toole was threatening one of his favorite teachers. Mr. O'Toole received a police escort out of the building and was taken to a local precinct, where he was locked up until later that day when he was presented with an order of protection, restraining him from direct contact with Jill.

Most important, I kept my promise to Jill.

She subsequently broke up with her boyfriend and moved in with her aunt.

At the graduation ceremonies, she proudly received an employee's achievement award from McDonalds.

✳✳✳

After graduation from the Fashion Institute of Technology, Jill accepted a position as an assistant designer at Macy's Department Store.

Later that year, Mr. O'Toole, piloting his motorcycle at an excessive rate of speed, broadsided an unoccupied passenger vehicle.

He died instantly.

CHAPTER 11

Gratitude at Its Best

✳✳✳

There were times when my students, as tokens of their gratitude, would show their appreciation of my efforts in weird sorts of ways.

Representing our school and accompanied by my wife, Anne, and a number of students from the Retail Work Program, I attended a book fair held at the hall of the Board of Education; I was anxious to get the latter more involved in the ways of the social and business world.

In visiting the various booths, we gathered free material containing information that I felt would be useful to our program. I gave my car's trunk key to Robert Brenner who, with another student, volunteered to carry the material to the car, which was parked near the building.

Anne and I continued to walk around, observing and enjoying the exhibits.

I next saw Robert about thirty minutes later. He smiled and said, "Mr. Findling, there's a special treat in the trunk of your car, but to more thoroughly enjoy it, don't open the trunk until you get home."

The pleasantness of our stroll around the hall, enjoying the exhibits, was suddenly interrupted by a rather loud discussion between two soldiers in front of a U. S. Army recruiting booth, which was located between two exhibits.

Apparently one of the soldiers was very upset with his associate. I heard him say, "While I went to take a leak, you were so busy flirting with that chick in the next booth that someone stole the fucking typewriter from under our desk."

To which the other soldier replied, "Yeah, but that chick has a great ass. I got her phone number, and she has a friend."

I immediately looked for Robert and finally located him. I said, "Robert, remember the time you were working at Macy's, and I showed you an advertisement for a ladies handbag selling for fifty dollars that I wanted to purchase as a gift for my wife? I gave you the fifty dollars to buy it. The next day you appeared at my office with two items: the handbag and my fifty dollars. You said, 'This is my treat for having gotten me the job at Macy's'."

I asked him, "Do you remember how upset I was by your action, insisting that the way you brought the handbag out of the store is the way you should bring it back? Well, Robert, the same thing goes for the special treat in the trunk of my car. I thank you very much for your generous gift-giving thoughts. But within the next half hour, I expect to find the returned typewriter located either under or on top of the recruiters' desk."

I added, "Also, Robert, the invitation to the Rotary Club luncheon last week was an honor extended to our program. Their donation of two hundred dollars in support of our program definitely did not include the bottles of scotch and gin that mysteriously appeared in the desk drawer of my office subsequent to our visit. Robert, any of the above could have affected our program's reputation if you had been caught."

A half hour later, Anne and I found Robert sitting in front of the army recruiters' desk, answering questions that were being typed into "my" former typewriter. The questions were relevant to his enlisting in the army following graduation.

After graduation, Robert joined the army and eventually attended officer's candidate school. He retired as a commissioned officer after twenty-five years of service that included tours in Iraq and Afghanistan.

During a recent chance meeting with Robert at an alumni gathering, he reminded me of the fact that his positive life experience for the prior twenty-five years was a direct result of his returning the typewriter, and for that he was extremely grateful.

His follow-up hug was by far the best of all the treats.

CHAPTER 12

Help, I Love My Job

✷✷✷

Students in the Retail Work Program were always welcome to come to my office and discuss any situation, positive or negative, whether at home or at work.

This was the reason Susan appeared at my office on a Monday morning.

Originally placed through our program, for almost six months Susan had been employed as a salesperson in a local high-fashion store, Lawrence Ladies' Boutique, and was thoroughly enjoying her learning experience. This included talking to buyers and company sales representatives from Calvin Klein, Liz Claiborne, etc., who came to the store to discuss their seasonal products. Susan felt really good because the representatives would question her regarding customer buying habits and compliment her sales skills, as did her many satisfied customers.

She was, however, experiencing a problem. A few weeks earlier, Larry, the store owner and manager, started making inappropriate suggestive remarks that were increasing in nature and had begun to involve touching and excessive hugging.

Upon discussing this with a fellow employee, Susan ascertained that about a year earlier, an employee in a sales position comparable to Susan's had experienced similar problems with Larry and told him how uncomfortable he was making her feel. She was terminated for a number of reasons the following week.

Susan said, "I really love my job, but I do not want this harassment to continue, and I don't know how to approach Larry without the possibility of being terminated. Please tell me what to do."

I said, "Susan, report to work tomorrow, and I assure you that by then, the problem will be resolved without your fear of losing your job."

I visited the store that afternoon, and after exchanging pleasantries with Larry, I listened to his enthusiastic comments regarding Susan's job performance.

I then told Larry a concocted story about Susan's phantom cousin, Joey, a former student and self-appointed family guardian. I said, "Larry, this kid is such a nut job that he confronted his sister Angie's boss, Antonio, who was sexually harassing Angie.

"Well, he beat the shit out of that pervert so badly that Joey was arrested, served time in jail, and was finally released two weeks ago. Larry, when Joey visited my office at school last week, I happily informed him that his favorite cousin, Susan, was doing extremely well in school and had a great part-time job as a salesperson for a famous boutique on Steinway Street. 'In fact,' I told him, 'her boss, Larry, is like a father to her.' But Larry, please don't bring up Joey's name to Susan. She doesn't like to talk about her cousin and his infamous past."

Besides, Susan would have no idea who Larry was talking about.

From then on, Susan maintained a perfect business relationship with Larry, with her period of employment lasting more than two years.

Susan's interest in fashion design continued to the point where she graduated from the Fashion Institute of Technology.

✳✳✳

Five years after her date of employment at Alexander's Department Store, Susan was promoted from an assistant to a buyer's position, and then to assistant store manager.

What a move. So proud.

CHAPTER 13

Lou, Diana Ross, and Moishe

***

One Friday morning, sitting at my desk and waiting for my double-period class to arrive for their final exam, I was approached by Lou Springer, a star football player at our school.

Lou's possibility of receiving a college scholarship was partially based on improvement of his grades. Although his test marks and class participation were at a passing level, I had given Lou a failing grade for the first half of the term. This was based on the fact that he had cursed and used foul language, for which I had zero tolerance. If used, it would qualify a student for an automatic failure. When used during the second and final half of the term, there could be no reprieve.

Lou informed me, "My test average is ninety or better, I have participated willingly in class discussions, and most important, Mr. Findling, I haven't said one fuckin' curse word during this entire second half."

I said, "Lou, I assure you that if you do well in the final exam, you will be rewarded."

We also agreed that if Lou spotted me fifteen points (twenty-one points would win) in an after-school paddleball game in the schoolyard and won the game, five points would be added to his final test mark.

"Just to change the subject, Lou, could you let me in on a little secret?"

"For you, Mr. F, anything. What do you want to know?"

"Where is the rest of the class?"

"They think you're absent.

The Long Island Expressway was a parking lot that morning, contributing to my late arrival. And that is why my car's absence from its usual spot was immediately noticed by students arriving early, especially those who were ill prepared for the test awaiting them.

The rumor spread. Mr. Findling is absent! Deliverance and hallelujah! *No test!!* Off to Moishe's, the corner luncheonette, and its jukebox, featuring Diana, Michael, the Temptations, and all. Marvin *Gaye* was substituting for Marvin *Findling.*

So the above was the obvious reason why Lou and two other students were the only ones present when class was to begin.

I called on Lou's athletic ability by dispatching him on a mission-to count the number of students from our class who were celebrating my absence at Moishe's. My spy returned in record time and informed me that at least twenty students from our class were at the luncheonette.

After careful thought, about thirty seconds, I came up with a great plan-subject to Moishe's approval. I called and explained the situation to Moishe, who laughingly agreed to close the store for forty-five minutes, thus offering the surprised students the opportunity of completing the test while being entertained by the Supremes ("Baby Love," "Stop in the Name of Love") and the Jackson Five on the store jukebox.

Lou, the two other students, and I began our pilgrimage with the testing materials to Moishe's, arriving in less than ten minutes.

On with the test!

At the conclusion of the test and prior to our exodus from Moishe's, I informed the students of my paddleball agreement with Lou and told them they would also have five points added to their test mark if Lou won.

More than twenty students showed up at the schoolyard that afternoon to witness the epic event. By some miracle, I added one point to my total, but to the students' and Lou's delight, I lost the game 21–16.

Another spectator at the game was the school principal. He said to me, "You could be receiving an unsatisfactory write-up in your permanent record for conducting a classroom activity off school grounds. Also, my eight-year-old daughter is a better paddleball player than you."

My follow-up thought regarding this latter comment was that the principal should commit an unnatural sexual act upon himself. However, I didn't outwardly express this feeling for two reasons.

First, because of my foul language edict, I didn't want Lou to consider me a hypocrite. Second, the principal, an excellent humorist, was one of my favorite people.

Lou received his college scholarship and subsequently played professional football in Canada.

CHAPTER 14
Raymond and Me

✳✳✳

During my many years as an educator, I would invariably encounter students who commented that certain subjects were boring and meaningless to their future.

As coordinator of the Retail Work Program, I continually attempted to develop special curricula, the latest being consumer education, directed at creating more student interest and increasing their desire to learn. Two other courses, business and criminal law, remained very popular and meaningful, since many of the students could be facing a future in either business or crime. The three courses continued to attract guest speakers from the local police precinct, lawyers, stockbrokers, and the local banks.

Of my many teaching experiences, the following is one of my most unforgettable. Raymond Treadwell was an African American student taking the criminal law class. Noticeable about Raymond was his attire, which included wearing a starched white shirt and black bow tie every day. His punctuality and attendance records were 100 percent.

For the first third of the term, Raymond stared straight ahead during the entire class period, without displaying any apparent interest in the subject matter, always maintaining the same blank expression, his eyes never meeting mine or those of the guest speakers. Similar to his lack of participation in classroom discussions, he never questioned any of the speakers, an important part of their presentations.

However, contrary to the above, his test marks averaged 90 percent. His responses to subjective test questions were thought provoking. Also, many times he would approach my desk after class and would comment or have a question regarding subject matter discussed during class while still avoiding eye contact.

I ascertained during one of those occasions that we both had a follow-up free period, and I asked him to remain a little longer and perhaps answer a few questions that were on my mind. He reluctantly agreed.

I asked him, "Raymond, do you find something wrong with my subject matter presentations? Considering your lack of class participation, this is in direct contrast to your approaching me after class to discuss the lesson."

Raymond said, "I look forward to attending your class every day, because it is my favorite and is deeply influencing my desire to eventually enter the field of law. However, I am a member of the Black Muslim faith. Our philosophy is that the white man is the devil in disguise. That's why I don't look at you. I don't want to be influenced by the white man's teachings, which are mainly detrimental to blacks and beneficial to whites. Therefore, my positive interest in the subject matter, inspired by you, the devil, is having a very disturbing influence on me, since it contradicts my faith's beliefs."

Adding a touch of humor to our conversation, I told Raymond there was an occasion after a sexual interlude when a former girlfriend of mine remarked, "Marvin, you are such a devil."

I then said, "Religious beliefs are a very delicate issue and must be confronted by the individual's inner self. My own personal feelings are that you, Raymond—whether because of your attendance, appearance, or test grades—are by far the best student in the class, and you could be even better if you would contribute to classroom discussions, whether you wanted to look at me or not."

Evidently, our private discussion had a positive effect. During the second third of the semester, Raymond would occasionally ask questions and comment when called on. During the final third, he was all gung ho, smiling away, and became the major contributor to classroom discussions. He also assigned himself the task of becoming the in-house defense attorney during the mock trials performed when our guest speaker was a local attorney.

At no time did we discuss the reasoning for his change in attitude. This being his senior year, Raymond awarded me the honor of being the first person to sign his yearbook.

I was one of the members of the faculty sitting on the stage during the graduation ceremonies. After he received his diploma and a handshake from the principal, Raymond, looking directly at me, approached and gave me a hug that brought tears to our eyes.

Some years later, in the middle of a teaching period, there was a knock on the classroom door. I opened the door, and there was Raymond, in uniform. He informed me that he was completing his tour of duty with the army and had been accepted by the John Jay School of Criminal Justice for the following semester.

I received another hug, right in front of the class.

After his graduation from New York Law School, Raymond was appointed to the position of public defender by the City of New York.

CHAPTER 15

Alberto's Visit

✳✳✳

On a typical school day, based on incorrect room information, who should appear at the office of the Retail Work Program (RWP) but none other than Mr. Alberto Lopez, noted TV reporter, with a cameraman in tow. Alberto was there to interview Mr. Mel Banks, coordinator of SPARK, the very successful school drug-awareness program. He was greeted by three students, Maurice Richardson, Luis Pagano, and Alex Reilly, who had earlier been aimlessly spending their free period occupying the office.

But now, having been forewarned by security of Mr. Lopez's arrival, they concocted a story that would make better use of their time and insure an escape from boredom.

When asked by Alberto to inform Mr. Banks of his arrival, the students stared at him with looks of dismay. After securing Alberto's promise not to reveal the source, the students offered some shocking information relative to Mr. Banks.

Alex said, "Mr. Banks is involved in a terrible school scandal that the administration is trying to keep within the confines of the school."

Luis said, "He has been accused of having sexual relations with an underage student after plying her with drugs, and a rumor is circulating that she's pregnant as a result of their tryst."

"Also," said Maurice, "Mr. Banks has recently appeared in some rather sexually explicit photos involving him, the cheerleaders captain, and the school's star quarterback. His position as coordinator of the drug program has been terminated, and he is being replaced by Mr. Marvin Findling."

Continuing to stretch the figments of his imagination, Maurice said, "We'll try to locate Mr. Banks, but we may not be successful, because he arrived at school this morning in an alcoholic state, which lately has been a common occurrence, and was told by the principal to go home. But don't worry. If we're not successful in finding Mr. Banks, then we'll inform Mr. Findling of your arrival."

Luis told Alberto, "While you wait, why don't you make yourself comfortable and light up a joint? But please open the window and keep the door closed, because we don't want Mr. Findling to see or smell anything funny."

While salivating over the sensational story he had fallen upon, Alberto and his cameraman waited for either Mel, me, or the three students to return, but to no avail. Alberto was finally informed by a student, dispatched by Mel, that he was in the wrong office, and that Mr. Banks was still awaiting his interview. During this entire period of time, I was busy teaching, completely unaware of the above happenings.

The three students (apparitions), possibly future candidates for Academy Awards, continued their search, which actually never began, for Mr. Banks and Mr. Findling. I was finally made aware of the prank almost two months later, at graduation ceremonies, when the trio confessed their transgression in detail while happily realizing a time for retribution was past tense.

Embarrassment alone kept Alberto from reporting his experience beyond the interview with Mel, which went very well. The SPARK program was successfully reported as one of the best run in the city.

✳✳✳

Alex, Luis and Maurice, attended Pace University, proudly receiving BBA degrees in Finance.

The three eventually became stockbrokers, but none with the "Wolf of Wall Street" because of their negative(?) feelings about misrepresentation.

Mothers, Daughters, and Tradition

***

The following is an example of personal problems that were discussed in my office with students from the Retail Work Program.

On a Friday morning, Susan Chan walked into my office, sat down, and with tears in her eyes said, "My father is the owner of a Chinese hand laundry. We live in an apartment above the store. Yesterday, two men came into the apartment through an open window and raped my mom, one or the other keeping a hand over her mouth to keep her from crying out. My father was completely unaware of what was happening.

"After they were finished, they warned my mom not to call the police, or they would return and rape her again, or her daughter, who they had seen at times helping in the store. But if she didn't report anything, they would not come back. When she went downstairs and told my father what had just happened, he reprimanded her for leaving the window open and sent her back upstairs. When I came home from school and walked into the apartment, my mother broke down and told me what happened. I went downstairs to the store and confronted my father. 'Mom just told me what happened. Why didn't you call the police?'

61

"Dad said, 'Your mother's carelessness has brought disgrace upon our family, and I am too embarrassed to call the police.'

"I said, 'You have to call the police, or at least bring Mom immediately to a hospital to be examined, because these guys might have a disease.'

"He said, 'I'm not leaving the store, I'm not taking your mother to a police station, and I'm not taking her to a hospital. Enough shame has been brought upon our family. You should respect your father's decision and not tell him what he has to do.'

"Still confronting my father, I said, 'I understand Chinese tradition about fatherdaughter respect, and coldness regarding personal feelings, but I do love Mom and you very much. So if you don't take her to a police station, I'm going to. Also, she has to be examined.'

"Dad then said, 'You are no longer to be considered a member of the family because of your lack of respect for me and my decision.'

"I responded, 'As I told you before, I do love you. But if that's how unconcerned you are about the health and safety of my mother—your wife—then you can take your decision and stick it up your ass.'

"My mother still refuses to go to the police station without my father's permission. Fuck tradition. Last night, I moved out. I pray for my mom. My heart is broken."

Listening to Susan's story was so heartrending that when she suddenly burst into tears, I wanted to cry along with her.

From the beginning of this family tragedy, her father's attitude was disturbing. This child should have been consoled, not lectured, which made her emotionally an additional victim of the rape. The father, because of his selfish lack of consideration and support, was a major negative factor.

My best contribution at the time, in attempting to point Susan in the right direction, was to emphasize that her mother should be examined.

However, I could not offer other opinions, because I felt they would only be construed as additional negative contributions to the family breakdown. I actually had thoughts of personally going to the store that afternoon and confronting the son of a bitch.

About one week later, Susan informed me that her mother was examined and tested at an independent medical facility, where they found no injury or disease.

At the graduation ceremonies, attended by her mom, Susan received an award from The Future Business Leaders of America (FBLA).

✳✳✳

Susan graduated from St. John's University and is currently employed as an assistant producer with the MTV network.

Susan still sees her mom, but has never returned home.

CHAPTER 17

Adventures with Mikey

***

Open-school night at a public high school is an interesting event. The primary purpose is to have parents visit individual teachers for a one-on-one discussion regarding their child's performance in that teacher's class.

You never know who will show up, and for what reason. For example, two parents came into my classroom, identifying themselves as Mr. and Mrs. Kapapoulas, she bawling up a storm, Mr. K trying to pacify her.

Mrs. K's opening remarks, hardly distinguishable through her crying, were, "Well, I guess you'll also tell us how our son, Mikey, is the worst student in your class, just like in all the others."

Actually, this was not exactly the case. Mikey, known to me as Michael, was not the worst student but runner-up, based on the fact that another student, Albert, although having a slightly higher test average than Michael's thirty-five, qualified to receive an F minus, as compared to Michael's F. This thoughtful decision was derived by considering that Albert's classroom behavior, entirely not subject related, was more disruptive. Michael, on the other hand, was content to spend his class time reading the sports section of the *Daily News*.

Upon observing Mrs. K's condition, it was not in my heart to reveal the above. Instead, I said, "Your son, Michael will be working on a project that will make him one of the best students I've ever had, and he **loves** to read. You should be very proud of him."

After Mrs. K questioned and was assured that we were talking about the same person, she walked out of the classroom, beaming.

Her husband, following close behind her, suddenly turned around, smiled at his newfound comrade in arms, with the universal arm-pumping gesture informing me that he would successfully score at his project that evening.

The next day, I detained Michael after class and informed him of his parents visit the prior evening and how heartbroken his mother was over the negative reports she was receiving from his other teachers. I said, "Michael, I was so touched by your mom's emotional condition—she was literally crying—that I actually lied to her about your class performance, telling her that you were one of my better students. This is very disturbing to me, and you and I must correct it. In other words, *we* are going to unlie the lie, and by the end of this semester, you will be the best—or close to the best—student in this class.

"Rather than sitting in the back of the room, you will now be sitting in the first seat of the row in front of me. Also, you can no longer be reading the sports section of the *Daily News*, because you can't bring the paper to class. So instead of staring at me for forty minutes every period, thinking of ways to make me disappear, you will get involved. Since this is a business law class, I'm assigning you two projects, each relating to your favorite subject, sports, and **our** favorite team, the **New York Yankees.** First, design an agreement between you, as an agent, and a fictional ballplayer, where for a predetermined compensation agreement, you will solely represent that player in contract negotiations with the Yankees or any other professional baseball team. Second, design a five-year guaranteed contract, including salary, options, etc., between the New York Yankees and the fictional ballplayer you, as his agent, will be representing.

"You can receive some help from Will Hadden, who I know personally. He's a sports reporter for the *Daily News*. His daughter goes to our school, and he has volunteered to offer some assistance. All additional research is up to you, and I'll assist you as best I can."

Michael was silent.

"Since baseball—especially the Yankees—is so special to you, I'm sure you'll enjoy the projects. Most important, you'll make your mother, father, me, and especially yourself proud of your effort. Michael, put your heart and soul into it, and your final grade will reveal the reward for your accomplishment."

By this time, I was starting to feel like a combination of Reverend Billy Graham and Bishop Fulton Sheen, about to finalize the above with a solid "Praise the Lord." But all I said was, "The reports are due by the end of May. Good luck."

Michael was actually able to contact an agent for a New York Yankees ballplayer, and he received all the help necessary for his two reports, which were turned in prior to the deadline. He actively participated in classroom activities, had the agent appear as a guest speaker, and received a ninety as his final grade.

After graduation, Michael went into partnership with his father in the restaurant business. He eventually opened his own restaurant in New York City, featuring half-pound Angus hamburgers and fresh-squeezed orange juice. The restaurant became so popular that it was written up in *Zagat*, the *New York Times*, and *New York Magazine*.

Michael's success story continues. He founded a home improvement business, and recently built a multi-million dollar mansion.

Michael, his mother and father, and various relatives have become dear friends of mine and remain so to this day.

CHAPTER 18

Stanley Smart – Part One

One of the most memorable students in the Retail Work Program was sixteen year-old Stanley Smart, sometimes stutterer and an extrovert or introvert, according to his mood swing.,

Stanley would spend at least one hour a day on our office phone, supposedly developing part-time jobs with local merchants for students in the program.

One day, I decided to have lunch in my office which was contrary to having it in the teacher's lounge. During that time period, Stanley, who was absent that day,.would normally be on the office phone, calling potential employers. I became aware of Stanley's other ventures when I picked up the phone's receiver and retrieved call-back messages from three different parties, all having been made during my prior teaching period.

Apparently, Stanley was successfully applying his skills to not only developing jobs, which included one for himself, but at the same time pursuing his other interests: betting on pro baseball and day-trading on the stock market.

All three parties thought that they were contacting Stan directly on his personal phone, based on the following messages:

1. "Stan the man, this is Louie. You are plus two dimes. The line on the Yankees is 9/11 with Ford, otherwise 7/8. Call back soon. The game starts in about two hours. Your call code is Stan for Cheech. Anything mysterious, hang up."

2. "Mr. Smart, this is Mr. Withers from Merrill Lynch. You are three days past the settlement date on your IBM purchase, and the stock is up two points today, but Pegasus Gold is down again on the negative news. You'll have to wire $2,500 by Friday afternoon at three o'clock to meet your margin requirements, or some of the IBM will be sold in order to meet fed regulations."

3. "Mr. Smart, this is Anne, from Bache. First, would you please stop coming on to me. You sound very cute, but you're too late. I'm already engaged. Also, Mr. Goldfarb, my manager, was very impressed with the ongoing telephone interview, relative to the research analyst position you inquired about. He was looking forward to setting up an appointment to meet you personally, but you ended the conversation by telling him, 'Go f-f-fuck y-y-yourself.' Mr. Goldfarb looked like he was about to have a stroke until you explained the reason for your explicit comment."

Stanley, a victim of Tourette's syndrome, had neglected to take his medicine that morning, which was the reason for his involuntary outburst.

Stanley, sometimes you're not so smart!

CHAPTER 19

Stanley Smart – Part Two

✳✳✳

When Stanley appeared in my office the next day, I was ready to start an interrogation worthy of the KGB and Gestapo combined.

Stanley sat down and said, "Mr. Findling, I know why you sent for me, and I'm ready to answer your questions before you even ask them. All of them.

"As per your instructions, this is my daily schedule. I take the employer list and telephone out of the locked drawer. I immediately try to meet your quota of developing two jobs a day, or ten for the week. Most times, I work around your canned pitch; at other times I use my personal approach.

"Lately, I've been getting more employment requests than usual. As you know, I got a call Monday from Alexander's for two cashiers, and a return call on Tuesday from Waldbaum's for a cashier. Also, Tuesday I had a telephone interview with a Mr. Goldfarb of Bache & Co. He was very impressed with my knowledge of the stock market and wants to interview me tomorrow regarding a possible position as an analyst trainee.

"The practice of role playing, when you play the part of the potential employer and then critique my telephone technique, really helps me when I make the actual phone calls; it allows me to meet and even surpass my weekly quota with time to spare. But these increased skills have allowed me the time to venture into a new business opportunity."

I raised an eyebrow.

"Stanley Smart Enterprises, operating out of the confines of this office, runs what is known as a 'six-hit pool,' which works as follows. Anyone, teachers excluded, can select three major-league ballplayers who they think will get a total of at least six hits that day. Games have to begin after 2:00 p.m. Minimum bet is a dollar. Maximum bet is five dollars. Odds are seven to one, so payout on a dollar is seven dollars. Bets must be received by me personally during the sixth period only at Mr. F's office, because that's when he's teaching. I have a list of excuses that students can use to get out of their sixth-period class so that they can come to my(?) office and make their bets. Example: 'I've got diarrhea. I **need** the pass.'"

He continued, "The students are also warned that if they happen to see Mr. Findling while on their way to my office, they should disappear or actually go to the bathroom. I've been using the money I was making to pay off my gambling debts and money owed the stockbroker. There have been days when I've pulled in more than one hundred dollars, hoping that no one wins the bet. Only Calvin Williams is making more than me, scalping tickets at the Knick and Ranger games. Well, that's it. You found me out. I guess you'll fail me and throw me out of the program, and I don't blame you. My increased telephone skills should have been used for the benefit of the Retail Work Program rather than my own selfish purposes. I let you down, and for that, I'm truly sorry."

I replied, "Stanley Smart Enterprises is officially out of business, as is our office phone number for your purposes. This afternoon, I want you to inform all your various business acquaintances—your bookie, stockbroker, or whoever—of your new phone number. It can be your home phone or any other number of your choosing. But not this number. Again, this number is out. Also, you are expelled from the office of the Retail Work Program until further notice, but not from the program. Excluding your touch of insanity, I have no reason to fail you. You are in a sales class, and you are a salesman par excellence."

I added, "But **I have** to see a parent, preferably your dad, by tomorrow. They can call me either at this number, which you are very familiar with, or through the school. Stan, you have a serious gambling problem. It has to be straightened out sooner rather than later. Otherwise, you may qualify as the first high school student ever to have the honor of being chased by a bookie, a loan shark, the Securities and Exchange Commission, or possibly Anne, from Mr. Goldfarb's office at Bache, informing you that she's pregnant.

"Based on your previous comments, I know and appreciate your true feelings about the Retail Work Program. But if I don't see one—or better yet, **both**—of your parents tomorrow, you will be expelled from the program and failed for the course. Then, just think! You can reacquaint yourself with those fuckin' idiots you used to hang out with before I accepted you into our program. Stan, you can be the best of the best, **and with your help**, I think it can happen."

We shook hands, and as he was about to leave the office, I had one final comment. "By the way, I like Thurman Munson, Willie McCovey, and Steve Garvey for the six hits."

I saw Stanley's parents the following day. He subsequently became one of the youngest members of Gamblers Anonymous.

✳✳✳

Stanley's interview with Mr. Goldfarb at Bache went very well, and he was hired on a part-time basis. After his graduation from Pace University with a BBA in finance, he was retained on a full-time basis as a research analyst.

He is currently a top producer in the sale of hedge funds with a major brokerage firm in Greenwich, Connecticut. His yearly earnings are in the seven-figure range.

Stanley, at other times, you're very smart.

As long as you keep remembering to take your medicine.

CHAPTER 20

A Day with James

✳✳✳

James Dunn was an all-city, first-team basketball player at Bryant High, with dreams of becoming a star point guard with the New York Knicks.

Although he was a constant twenty-point scorer in basketball, he was a zero-point scorer in classroom contribution, in homework, or in anything related to our subject matter. I informed James that his lack of contribution was leading toward a failing status for the first half of the term.

He said, "If l fail any of my subjects, I will be suspended from the team."

As a final opportunity, I gave him a minimal project, with a one-week deadline. Nothing. I then gave him a weekend extension. Again, zilch. James failed for the first half.

One day, during the beginning of the second half of the term, James walked up to the rear window of our classroom, which fortunately happened to be located on a lower floor, and addressed me.

"Due to low grades," he said, "I am about to be suspended from the team. Unless you promise me that I will get a passing grade for the second half, I am going to jump out of the window." He opened the window. "If anyone approaches me, or if you send for security, I will jump."

While this was happening, about thirty students sat quietly listening but staring straight ahead, because I immediately told them, "Anyone looking at James, or discouraging or encouraging him, will automatically fail for the second half."

I said, "James, I think you are not only good, but a great point guard, and it's a pleasure to watch you play. In fact, I even think there is the possibility of a college scholarship based on your basketball skills, and I want to help you achieve that goal. For that reason, last night I prepared and now want you to know the minimum requirements necessary for you to pass my course. A major portion is a project assignment based on your basketball knowledge.. However, James, if you do not intend to meet these simple requirements, then you might as well go out the window right now, as I will also fail you for the second half."

As an added inducement, I said, "James, since this is the last class of the day, and the period is about to end, I will do something special for you. I will give you some additional project credit if we immediately go to the school athletic field and indulge in a game of handball, with the provision that you have to win by at least five points."

James very enthusiastically agreed but then suddenly climbed out on the window ledge, stating that he was so excited regarding my proposal, "I have to pee, and I can't wait to get to the boys' room."

He proceeded to urinate from the window into the garden below, climbed back in, and closed the window.

"James, how can I pass you if you give me a heart attack?"

After I was able to catch my breath, James, on my insistence, stopped in the boy's room to wash his hands. Then, with about twenty excited students, he and I proceeded to the athletic field to indulge in the epic handball game. James won by a score of 21–2, qualifying him for immediate project credit.

About one week later, on a Sunday evening, James called me at home, and said, "My favorite aunt has passed away, and her Cadillac is up for sale. Since you are my favorite teacher, you have the option of buying the car before it is sold to a stranger. At least it doesn't look like that refugee from a junkyard that you drive around in."

My response was an inquiry as to whether he had completed my project assignment that weekend; his reply was an emphatic, **"YES"**

My final remark: "James, are you sure you're not *pissing* me?"

James, a very intelligent young man, passed all his subjects for the second half and graduated with a basketball scholarship offer from Southern Methodist University, which he gladly accepted.

A week after his graduation, I purchased the mint-condition Cadillac and kept it for five years.

Following his graduation from SMU, James received a ten day contract to play for a team in the National Basketball Association, but nothing permanent. He then played professional basketball in Europe for five years. Upon return to college and completion of his educational courses, James was hired as a health education teacher and basketball coach at a Dallas high school, a stone's throw from SMU.

CHAPTER 21

True Appreciation

✳✳✳

My classes in salesmanship, which were a part of the Retail Work Program, sometimes produced amazing results.

One day as I was leaving school, I had this consuming desire to see a New York Knicks basketball game that evening at Madison Square Garden. Knicks games were always a sellout, so I knew I would have to pursue various resources for obtaining a ticket. Calling on all my negotiating talents, I was prepared for the inevitable outcome—encountering the scalpers.

There were a few novices, but most were masters of the art. I was offered tickets valued at thirty-five dollars for fifty dollars and up, and tickets valued at seventy-five dollars for a hundred dollars and up. I was about to settle for a seat in the rafters, where an oxygen mask was a necessity.

Suddenly, I heard a voice bellowing from behind me, "Mr. Findling, Mr. Findling." I turned around, and who should I encounter but Calvin Williams, the dog-food gourmet (*see* "Pal's Pals").

Calvin said, "As a reward for being my favorite teacher, I am offering you a $250 courtside seat for the ridiculous price of a hundred dollars." He repeatedly assured me that the ticket wasn't counterfeit.

At that point, an associate scalper, who looked like the African American version of Hulk Hogan, interrupted Calvin's one-way conversation. "My deal is better than Calvin's. My seat is in the upper mezzanine, and it'll cost you a hundred dollars, but you'll have the opportunity of enjoying a little coke that I'll be cooking up as soon as the coast is clear, and at no additional charge."

Calvin responded, "Uncle Leroy, show some respect. I know this man. And I could just as soon light up a joint and offer him a toke, but I don't do that shit no more."

Leroy said, "I'm sorry, man. I didn't mean to dis you. Calvin is my favorite nephew. And he's not fucked up, like he was six months ago, when the school threw him out. Then they took him back and put him in a program where he can go to different classes every day with the same teacher."

Leroy, taking a respite from his scalping operation, continued, "Calvin says that one day he had to eat some dog food to save the teacher's ass, and he had to carry the teacher's dog, a big motherfucker, from the classroom to the street to take a shit. But Calvin says the teacher is his main man, because he's learning him to be a salesman, and also legal shit, like he can't get laid if the bitch says no. Calvin says he's saving all the money he can, selling these tickets, so he can go to college. He hasn't smoked weed once since he went back to school. At least he says so. Me and my old lady are very proud of him."

All during this time, Calvin kept smiling and enjoying his uncle's dialogue. Finally he said, "Uncle, how would you like to one day meet the teacher I keep telling you about?"

Leroy responded, "The way you talk about him, I sure would like to meet that motherfucker one day and shake his hand."At that point, I extended my hand and said, "Hello, Uncle Leroy. I'm the motherfucker."

Poor Leroy. He just stared at me without saying a word. We shook hands. Then he put hi massive arms around me and said in the softest tone, "Thanks for helping Calvin." I really thought he was about to cry.

Calvin said, "Mr. Findling, about those $250 seats I was going to *give* you for a hundred bucks. Well, they're yours, free. No charge. Gratis. I didn't pay a dime for them, and neither will you. Enjoy! I've already made over four hundred dollars from ticket sales tonight and still have three left, which is why you're my favorite teacher. Man, you taught, I listened. Now I'm a better salesman than you. But no more drug lectures, please? And wait until you find out who I hustled your ticket from."

I accepted the ticket offer, entered the arena, and was escorted to my courtside seat.

And who did I find sitting next to me? None other than Spike Lee, the famous movie director, wearing his famous orange T-shirt with the Knicks insignia.

Spike asked, "Why are you in this seat?"

My reply, "Someone gave it to me. Why do you ask?"

Spike said, "Well, while I was hanging around with some friends in front of the Garden's main entrance prior to game time, a young fellow walks up to us and asks if anyone has an extra ticket, which

I actually did have. Before I can reply, he comes up with this sob story. He says, 'My name is Maurice, and I love the Knicks. I was supposed to be going to my first Knicks game ever tonight with my uncle Thaddeus, who bought the tickets. I was supposed to meet him here. But sometimes, my uncle fucks up. After waiting here for almost two hours, I got nervous and called his house. I was told that Uncle Thaddeus wasn't showing, because he gave the tickets to someone else to pay off a gambling debt.' Maurice, displaying the most forlorn look, said, 'My uncle fucked up again.'.

Now, the extra ticket I had was courtside and I knew I could easily get my cost back from any of the scalpers because of its great location.

"It started to rain. I looked at Maurice again. He was wiping either rain or teardrops from his face. The poor kid looked desolate. This heartrending situation had to be resolved. I said, 'Maurice, take this ticket. It's courtside. Let's go, Knicks!'"

"And now, instead of Maurice, I see you. Were you sold this ticket?"

"No. Like I said, it was given to me. No charge."

"Obviously, Maurice is a scalper. So why would he give you this great seat when he could get at least five hundred dollars for it?"

"It was given as a token of appreciation," I said.

"Why, who are you to him?"

"I'm a high school teacher, and he is one of my students."

"You must be special for him to just hand you the ticket. What do you teach him anyway?"

"Calvin Williams, alias Maurice, is taking three courses: sales, criminal law, and business law."

"What's such a big deal about taking a sales course, which is a lot of bullshit, anyway?"

"Well, let's put it this way, Spike. He learned how to bullshit you out of your courtside ticket."

Spike said, "This is so funny, I could make a story out of it."

The seat was great, as was the game and the enjoyment of sitting and rooting alongside the Knicks's number-one fan.

Calvin graduated from Pace University with a BBA degree in finance. He is currently employed as a financial adviser with Morgan Stanley.

CHAPTER 22

A Weekend to Remember

✻✻✻

As part of the activities at Bryant High School, for a nominal cost, senior students were permitted to spend a weekend at a dude ranch, the Hunter Mountain Resort. They would be chaperoned by four teachers selected by the students.

Married chaperones could bring their families. In my case, I brought my wife, Anne, and two of our children, Bobby and Marie.

Anne, concerned with the welfare of the students, made sure I performed my chaperone duties to the nth degree. I was constantly checking rooms and patrolling halls. I also stationed myself at one of the two bars while Anne supervised the other one, our purpose being to see that no hard liquor was served to the students.

While standing at the bar, I was approached by a student, Carlos Lopez. He said, "Mr. F, some guy is trying to make a move on your wife at the other bar."

I replied, "Thanks for the information, Carlos, but I assure you that that Mrs. F can handle the situation without my help."

Within ten minutes, at least five other students came up to me and expressed their concern.

Carlos approached me again and said, "We're on the verge of picking this guy up and dumping him in the indoor pool."

I decided to walk over and save the poor soul.

Anne chased me away, saying, "Go back to your bar where you belong." She was upset that I had interrupted the fun she was having navigating through what was possibly the most outrageous of all pickup lines, including a helicopter that would be landing momentarily next to the bar to whisk Anne and her new friend to Las Vegas.

Within five minutes of the time that I temporarily returned to my room, there was a knock on my door. It was Carrie, another student, who wanted to borrow our fifteen-year-old son, Bobby, for about an hour so that "I can make a man of him." Despite Bobby's protestations, I declined her offer.

The same night, Carlos and our daughter Marie, age thirteen, won the disco contest. The prize was a weekend for two at the ranch.

Anne, anticipating the prospect of being whisked away on her new friend's helicopter, rejected the prize offer, but promised both Carlos and Carrie that they could accompany her, Bobby, and Marie on the helicopter journey to Las Vegas.

After graduation, Carlos enlisted and completed a distinguished career in the service of the US Army.

Carrie is currently happily employed as a New York City elementary school teacher.

Anne is still longingly awaiting the return of her friend and his helicopter.

And I'm still wondering what happened to the three additional teacher chaperones who were supposed to accompany us on the weekend venture.

CHAPTER 23

Pamela and Me

✳✳✳

Here I was, arriving at William Polk High School in the Bronx to be interviewed for the principal's position, accompanied by Pamela Jones, a student from the Retail Work Program. Actually, this was my second interview at the school, which meant that they were down to the final five surviving applicants—similar to the final four in the NCAA basketball finals.

The panel consisted of the out-going principal, the president of the parent-teacher association, a representative of the teachers' union, a teacher, the president of the student council, and a representative of the community school board.

Eighty percent of the student population at Polk was either African American or Hispanic, with the remaining twenty percent Caucasian and Asian. Therefore, the reviewing committee had previously requested that I bring two students, one of African American and the other of Hispanic descent, both of whom had personal classroom experiences with me, to respond to questions asked by the panel. Pamela was a combination of everything, including Asian blood, and was very proud of her ethnic background. I felt she was very cable of responding to all questions, adding additional comments when required, but also, unfortunately, at other times when not required.

Pamela had many family issues that involved my counseling her as well as members of her family. Any of these issues could have, but did not deprive her of being on the verge of graduating and being accepted at the John Jay School of Criminal Justice. During the three years of our relationship, Pamela looked upon me with extreme loyalty, respected our teacher-student relationship, but nevertheless considered herself my buddy.

The questions asked by the panel consisted of how I would handle complaints from students regarding teacher bias, racial disturbances, and class control; input regarding increasing math and reading levels; and how I would feel about being the principal of a school where only 10 percent of the student body and faculty were Caucasian. They then directed questions at Pamela, inquiring whether she had experienced any bias or racial incidents while in my classes. Pamela described two separate incidents that were successfully resolved without help from security or administration.

"His practice of resolving problems within the boundaries of the classroom—without requiring outside assistance and thereby avoiding disciplinary procedures—adds to Mr. Findling's popularity among the student population," said Pamela.

Pamela was complimented for her mature responses to the panel's questions. The principal then directed Tyrone, the president of the student council, to accompany Pamela to the teachers' lounge for refreshments while the interview continued.

Said Pamela, "Let's go, Tyrone. Show me what you've got."

After another half hour of repetitious questions, I felt that a majority of the panel, myself included, was hoping I would come up with a wrong answer. I began to wonder what happened to

Pamela. I asked for directions to the teachers' lounge, temporarily excused myself, and left the principal's office.

Upon entering the lounge, who should I find comfortably relaxed on a couch, studying each other's architecture? None other than Tyrone and Pamela. I told them that I hated to break up their interlude. They exchanged phone numbers. As we were returning to the principal's office, Pamela commented, "Mr. Marvin, these motherfuckers are playing you. You are the token honky."

I thanked her for her thoughts.

Immediately following our return to his office, I was informed by the principal—to my increasing disappointment—that the board was seriously considering my candidacy, but they had a few more questions. He commenced asking questions similar to the ones he had asked Pamela and me forty-five minutes earlier.

At that point Pamela, apparently upset at the repetitious questions, jumped up, stating, "Mr. Findling, you too good for these people. Tyrone told me that the principal just came back from a nervous breakdown. There is no class control, and police are called almost every day to prevent fighting in the school cafeteria. These people will drive you crazy. They're already driving me crazy. Let's get the fuck out of here, this shit-hole school, and the Bronx, because except for my new soul mate, Tyrone, the Bronx is fucked up. Let's get into your badass Cadillac, ride through Harlem, and return to a good school, where you're appreciated."

The only reactions we heard and saw while fleeing the office was the teachers' union rep yelling, "Way to go, girl," and Tyrone applauding.

There was little communication between Pamela and me during our return trip to Bryant until we were driving along 125th Street in Harlem. When we passed a millinery shop, Pamela asked me to park the car, stating she wanted to go into the store to make a special purchase. She came out of the store, holding a bag. It contained a big purple hat. She placed the hat on my head and said, "You are now officially my pimp, which is better than being principal of that shit hole." Pamela started to cry. We hugged and returned to our school.

Because of family financial hardship, Pamela was forced to attend college on a part-time basis. But her fortitude paid off. She received her law degree from Fordham University and is currently employed as a legal aid attorney in Trenton, New Jersey.

CHAPTER 24

My Moment of Glory – Maybe

✳✳✳

A selected group of students from our Retail Work Program were to appear with me at the great hall of the Board of Education before top executives of the board, including principals, district superintendents, and the chancellor himself. The students were to discuss individual accomplishments that had been achieved through our program.

While traveling to the board that morning, we reviewed possible questions and student responses.

Susan, eager to discuss her experience with customers and buyers based on her sales position obtained through the program, intended to become a buyer. She had recently applied to, and had been accepted by the Fashion Institute of Technology.

Vermel was to explain how she was about to be employed as a provisional management trainee by the local Radio Shack, subject to her graduation.

Mikey was attempting to arrange an interview with the New York Yankees for a position as an apprentice team statistician. This was based on the fact that he had completed a statistical project on the players' salaries, supporting some and disputing others. He sent the report to the Yankees office and received a very complimentary response.

Raymond, the star of the criminal law class, planned to study and eventually practice law after completion of his army duty.

Pamela—our program's headhunter and job recruiter, and my personal advocate—intended, after college graduation, to either seek a position at or open her own employment agency.

Stanley, who was already working part time at Bache & Company, the Wall Street brokerage firm, was looking forward to a successful career in the financial world.

I asked Stanley, "Did you take your medicine this morning?"

His reply: "Yes, I did."

The students' presentations were great. Almost all questions were answered to the satisfaction of the questioners. Many compliments were given and happily received.

Not exactly in accordance with our original plan, Stanley stood up and thanked everyone for extending the invitation. He then looked directly at the superintendent of the Queens borough, a classy-looking lady if ever there was one, mentioned how uplifting this meeting was to all of us, shook her hand, and stated, "Thanks again, you fuckin' bitch!"

Stanley, a victim of Tourette's syndrome, had *once again* neglected to take his medicine.

CHAPTER 25

Beyond All Expectations

✳✳✳

As previously mentioned, included in the curriculum of the Retail Work Program was a course in salesmanship.

As part of the term project, but also as a hands-on approach, each student was required to demonstrate newly developed skills by selling at least one of the two hundred pocket calculators that were supplied on consignment by the local Radio Shack. The retail price per calculator was ten dollars.

Our indebtedness to Radio Shack for each calculator sold was three dollars. Of the seven dollars profit, the student could keep four dollars. The remaining three dollars would be added to a surplus fund, the project's profit. The fund would be controlled by a committee of ten students from the Retail Work Program, with myself as coordinator. A bonus of one hundred dollars was to be awarded to the student selling the most calculators during that period of time.

I estimated that with thirty-two students in the sales class, each student would sell one or maybe two calculators in order to meet the project requirement. A minimum of $200 would then go into the surplus fund, which would be spent at the committee's discretion.

The project began on October 1, with a final date of December 8.

Making me very proud was the fact that through their combined efforts, all the students met their individual requirement. In fact, some went far beyond.

Ellen sold one hundred calculators through her church, donating half her profits to the church.

Tommy picked up 150 additional calculators from Radio Shack and sold them all that weekend from a stand that he set up on Steinway Street. Based on a complaint from a local store merchant, he was chased by a gendarme for peddling without a license.

Marie sold fifty calculators through the local Elks Lodge and another fifty through the Rotary Club.

The sales momentum continued to the point where Radio Shack had to request additional supplies from their warehouse.

The most individual sales were by Vermel. She sold two hundred calculators at a reduced price of two for nineteen dollars from a stand at a local flea market, plus an additional fifty to relatives and social acquaintances.

All told, more than six hundred calculators were sold, resulting in a total of $1,800 going into the surplus fund, less the hundred-dollar bonus earned by Vermel, the winner of the contest.

A unanimous decision was then reached as to how to spend the profits. We immediately rented a hall, hired a disc jockey and caterer, and extended invitations to the principal, teachers, students, and their parents to attend a gala Christmas Eve celebration at the Steinway Street Manor, hosted by the Retail Work Program. The honored guests were the members of the Steinway Street Merchants Association, the employers of at least fifty students from our program.

Another honored guest was Mr. Robert Winston, the Radio Shack store manager, who presented Vermel with an additional hundred-dollar reward certificate. In fact, Mr. Winston was so impressed with Vermel's initiative that he hired her for a part-time sales position. Upon graduation, she was retained on a full-time basis. Her path of progress in both education and with Radio Shack continued. She attended evening classes at Baruch College and graduated with a BBA degree in marketing and sales management. At the same time, she was promoted to the position of store manager with Radio Shack.

I remain so proud of her.

And What an Ending –
THE WINNERS

✳✳✳

Ninety percent of the students seen in the above picture had a parttime job secured through the Retail Work Program, 100 percent graduated, and 90 percent attended college.

Author's Note

*** ✳✳✳

Because of its curricula and job opportunities, the Retail Work Program became so popular that it became one of the most sought after elective programs in the school, and eventually included some main stream (mentioned in some chapters) and honor students.

However, due to limited space, priority for acceptance into the program was always awarded to the former losers, for whom it was originated in the first place. For anyone else, it was a lottery pick.

Testimonials

(STUDENT)

THE RETAIL WORK PROGRAM AND ME (JAY V. RODRIGUEZ)

I first came into contact with Marvin Findling as a junior in high school at William Cullen Bryant High School in Astoria, Queens. One of my earliest memories of Marvin was that the students at school who knew him all seemed to like him. Case in point, a student I was having trouble with, who was giving me the stink eye whenever I ran into him—which meant we would eventually have to fight if we couldn't avoid one another—was playing paddleball with Marvin on one of the school courts...seemingly the only one without broken glass on it. This was the seventies in New York, mind you, and school funding was at the bottom of the city's budget woes. Anyway, Marvin beat him handily and afterward noticed I was watching. We said hello through the fence, and then he introduced me to my would-be nemesis...and lo and behold, that kid and I turned out to be friends. That pretty much encapsulates what was to follow when I enrolled in Marvin's Retail Work Program class. Every year he took on an assorted bunch—from good students to urchins—introduced those kids to a bigger world, and put a positive result on it.

In my specific case, I first met Marvin through my high school sweetheart. Marvin and I instantly clicked, and for the first time in my life, I had a male teacher who was not just a teacher but a mentor, a father figure, and most of all, a friend. Marvin encouraged me to join his program, which I knew had helped other kids, and most important, all those kids seemed happy and had a sense of success about them. So I joined in the spring term of my junior year, and it changed my life for the better. I was taken in by Marvin and the other kids in his program as a generally happy, intelligent, but middling student who was somewhat on the shy side and came out by the end of my senior year as a different person. I went from stuttering and stammering and being unsure of myself in front of groups to speaking in front of students and adults alike, such as professional groups of businessmen to Board of Ed dignitaries, without skipping a beat. I went from a midseventies average and ended my senior year at an eighty-eight average. I was able to get a partial scholarship to Pace University, from which I graduated at age twenty with a BBA in business management. Subsequently, I was able to attend the NYU Stern School of Business for the MBA program in finance/statistics. In the meantime, I was able to get a prestigious position with IBM when I graduated college. All of that was possible thanks to the foundation that was given to me by the Retail Work Program and Marvin. I learned to comport myself professionally for work and for life in general through the program. All the participants in the Retail Work Program were taught basic and advanced skills most kids never learned about, such as how to interview properly, how to be a professional in a work environment, how to budget, how to set goals, etc. In short, we learned skills that would help us for the rest of our lives.

Today, almost forty years later, I still am actively engaged with Marvin. He is still a mentor, a father figure, a teacher, and most important, a friend in whom I confide with my deepest life issues. I know I am not the only student of Marvin's with whom he has such a relationship, and it is a testament to the legacy he left on the kids he influenced through the Retail Work Program. Today I look back on those high school years, and I am ever so grateful for the day I met Marvin and for the blessings our friendship has brought me.

Wigglesworth C-21
Harvard College
Cambridge, Mass. 02138
January 31, 1975

Mr. M. Findling
William Cullen Bryant High School
48-10 31 Avenue
Long Island City, N.Y. 11103

Dear Mr. Findling,

I want to tell you that I am extremely grateful for the assistance that you and the Retail Work Program gave me during my years at high school. The job that I received from the program enabled me to work with different types of people, meet many people under a novel circumstance (salesman to customer), and it helped teach me the necessary responsibilities for college. The Retail Work Program gave genuine information on actual retail and business situations so I was better prepared to work in retailing than most of my co-workers.

The money I received as a result of the Retail Work Program and subsequent job allowed me to pay for my immediate college expenses (application fees and traveling expenses to visit the schools). It financed my high school prom tickets and the other senior activities, and more importantly, I was able to aid my family by contributing a portion of my pay to the household.

In looking for a part-time job at college I have the advantage of possessing the knowledge of how retailing operates and I've found that there are many jobs for those who have this knowledge.

The Retail Work Program at Bryant gives students an incentive to go to school and to receive what they feel school should supply; that is practical training that can be used through their lives after school. This program provides this invaluable training in the form of classroom and on the job business and retailing experiences. This is the great benefit of the program..

Again Mr Findling, I congratulate on the accomplishments of this program.

Sincerely,

Lawrence D. Mungin

Lawrence D. Mungin
Harvard College, Class of '79

Michael Randolph Gachotte
25-33 95th Street
East Elmhurst, N.Y. 11369
March 25, 1976

To Mr. Marvin Findling
(Job Coordinator of the Retail Work Course)

I would like to extend my deep thanks and appreciation
to you and the retail work course. The job you got me really
promoted a feeling of importance for both my family and I.

The retail work course itself gives young people a
good opportunity to explore the business world and gain
experience which they could never get in school. The young
people who take this course develope a maturity which is
often absent from the older generation. These same young
people are responsible and trustworthy also.

The retail work course made me realize the importance
of not only finishing high school but getting the highest
grades possible. To get a job a prospective employee must
be qualified to do the job and a high school graduate who
has had experience and good grades could easily be hired. The
retail work course certainly prepares a high school student
for better jobs in the future.

The best part about the retail work course is that
while gaining all this valuable experience, a student is
also earning his own paycheck. This is the big plus for any
student.

Once again I would like to thank Mr. Marvin Findling
for helping me in high school through his course. I have a
brother who will be taking retail work next term and I am
sure that you will help him also.

Your student,

Michael Gachette

Michael Gachette

Testimonials

(EMPLOYER)

STEINWAY STREET MERCHANTS ASSOCIATION, INC.

"The Longest Department Store in the World"

DEC 1 7 1979

24-27 STEINWAY STREET
ASTORIA, N.Y. 11103

RAvenswood 8-7535

Executive Secretary
ELISE MARTOCCI

December 14, 1979.

Mr. Martin Ilivicky, Principal.
William Cullen Bryant High School
48th Street and 31st Avenue
Astoria, New York 11103.

Dear Sir,

As we enter the holiday season, the merchants of Steinway Street would like to take this opportunity to thank you for your invaluabye assistance. Unlike other areas throughout the city, Astoria enjoys a very happy and comfortable relationship with the students of our local high school and this must be due, in large measure, to your helmsmanship.

I must also include a large measure of appreciation for Mr. Marvin Findling. For the past six years, Mr. Findling has been our prime source of supply for the part-time labor pool that we require. I have yet to hear one complaint from over 200 merchants that he services, which would indicate that he takes an inordinate interest in the individual, in order to avoid a mismatch. The Steinway community of businesspeople salutes his dedication and looks forward to supporting the proposed establishment of a pilot retail store in our trading area, run and financed entirely by the students of Bryant. Since September of this year, Mr. Findling has been investigating the possibility and looks to the future with a great deal of anticipation. With him at the forefront, it can't miss.

With all good wishes for a Happy and Healthy Holiday season, and again, thanks for Mr. Findling, I remain,

Sincerely yours,

JULIAN WAGER,
President.

"To foster trade on Steinway Street and to promote the Welfare of Astoria"

217

Alexander's

58TH STREET & LEXINGTON AVENUE, NEW YORK, N.Y. 10022 • 583-C

October 12, 1977

Mr. Marvin Findling
William Cullen Bryant
48-10 31st Avenue
Long Island City, N.Y.

Dear Marvin,

I just want to thank you for your continuing efforts in helping us fill the many available positions at Alexander's Lexington Avenue Store.

Your students have proven to be pleasant, enthusiastic employees, well qualified for starting positions such as cashiers, wrappers, sales, and stock. Furthermore, quite a few of your students have taken advantage of advancement opportunities and progressed, upon graduation, into our Executive Training Program. At least two of these, Karen Mathis, and Bertha Warren, have been promoted to even higher positions and are currently members of our Junior Executive team!

With a track record this good, I'm looking forward to maintaining our employment relationship well into the future.

Respectfully yours,

Richard Calgie
Asst. Personnel Manager
Alexander's Department Store of Lex. Ave. Inc.
731 Lexington Avenue
New York, N.Y. 10022

RC:ac

111

Established 1919

Tel. RA 8-$\left\{\begin{array}{l}2777\\2260\end{array}\right.$

Saymel's

COATS – SUITS – DRESSES
RAINCOATS – GOWNS – SPORTSWEAR
30-48 STEINWAY STREET
LONG ISLAND CITY, N. Y. 11103

May 24, 1974

Dear Mr. Findling,

    I am writing this letter in order to commend your job program.

    Based on my experience with our part-time employees currentley enrolled in your program, I think it is an excellent credit to the school, the business, the community, you and most of all the student.

    I wish you continued success in this fine program.

Sincerely,

Melvin Saler
President

MS:em

**Employer Ratings
for Students in the
Retail Work Program**

NAME *Maria Fernández*   DATE 12/19/77

SCHOOL *WC BRYANT H.S.*   WORK WEEK *Dec. 77*

FIRM *Alexander's*

1. COURTESY	5	5. APPEARANCE 5
2. COOPERATION AND LOYALTY	5	6. ABILITY TO FOLLOW INSTRUCTIONS 5
3. WILLINGNESS TO WORK	5	7. JOB PERFORMANCE 5
4. ATTENDANCE	5	*8. PUNCTUALITY 5

REMARKS *Maria is an exceptional worker. She has been very helpful in assisting us in demonstration and sell of toys. Very quick to learn, easy going and the customer's love her.*

TO BE RATED ON A SCALE OF 1 TO 5

5	EXCEPTIONAL
4	ABOVE AVERAGE
3	AVERAGE
2	BELOW AVERAGE ——— FAILING
1	EXTREMELY POOR

* ATTENDANCE
- NO ABSENCES = 5
- 2 ABSENCES = 4
- 3 ABSENCES = 3
- 4 ABSENCES = 2
- 5 ABSENCES = 1

* PUNCTUALITY
- NO LATENESS = 5
- 2 LATENESS = 4
- 3 LATENESS = 3
- 4 LATENESS = 2
- 5 LATENESS = 1

RED AS ONE ABSENCE.

Delano Anderson
SUPERVISOR'S SIGNATURE

Maria C. Fernández
STUDENT'S SIGNATURE

203

RATING SLIP   713

COOPERATIVE EDUCATION BUREAU

NAME *FREDDY SALAZAR*   DATE 1/4/78

SCHOOL *BRYANT High School*   WORK WEEK *Dec '77*

FIRM *ALEXANDER'S STORE Lex. 59 St*

1. COURTESY	5	5. APPEARANCE	5
2. COOPERATION AND LOYALTY	5	6. ABILITY TO FOLLOW INSTRUCTIONS	5
3. WILLINGNESS TO WORK	5	7. JOB PERFORMANCE	5
4. ATTENDANCE	5	*8. PUNCTUALITY	5

REMARKS *Outstanding, intelligent and efficient worker. Able to accomplish many job assignments in a short time, timely, works hard, cheerfully completes all job assignments.*

TO BE RATED ON A SCALE OF 1 TO 5

5	EXCEPTIONAL
4	ABOVE AVERAGE
3	AVERAGE
2	BELOW AVERAGE ——— FAILING
1	EXTREMELY POOR

* ATTENDANCE ✓
- NO ABSENCES = 5
- 2 ABSENCES = 4
- 3 ABSENCES = 3
- 4 ABSENCES = 2
- 5 ABSENCES = 1

* PUNCTUALITY
- NO LATENESS = 5
- 2 LATENESS = 4
- 3 LATENESS = 3
- 4 LATENESS = 2
- 5 LATENESS = 1

NY CONSECUTIVE ABSENCE SHOULD BE CONSIDERED AS ONE ABSENCE.

*Mr. N. Grippi
593-0880 ext. - 264*

431-60M-7-73   134   286
240-237

SUPERVI

STUDE

Additional Testimonials

THE COUNCIL
OF
THE CITY OF NEW YORK
CITY HALL
NEW YORK, N. Y. 10007
566-8046

PETER F. VALLONE
COUNCILMAN, 20TH DISTRICT, QUEENS
22-55 31ST STREET
LONG ISLAND CITY, N. Y. 11105
274-4984

COMMITTEE MEMBER:
CHARTER AND
  GOVERNMENTAL OPERATIONS
ENVIRONMENTAL PROTECTION
HEALTH
PUBLIC SAFETY

January 6, 1978

Martin Ilivicky, Principal
William Cullen Bryant High School
48th Street and 31st Avenue
Long Island City, N. Y. 11103

Dear Martin:

      Thank you for your recent letter concerning your very successful Retail Work Preparation Program at Bryant.

      I am very favorably impressed and I think that Marvin Findling, the teacher who brought your program to life and is making it flourish, is an outstanding example of the kind of dedicated people that will also bring new life to our beleaguered city.

      Congratulations to him and to you for your leadership and supervision.

          Cordially,

          PETER F. VALLONE

PFV:af
CC: Marvin Findling

Mr. Findling
Well Done!

BOARD OF EDUCATION
THE CITY OF NEW YORK
———
WILLIAM CULLEN BRYANT HIGH SCHOOL
48TH STREET AND 31ST AVENUE
LONG ISLAND CITY, N. Y. 11103

MARTIN ILIVICKY
PRINCIPAL

721-5404

June 23, 1977

Mr. Marvin Findling

Dear Marvin:

As the year draws to a close, I wish to thank you for the
excellent work you have been doing in our Retail Work Program.
The success of our "earn and learn" experience has helped make
us a leading school in the city in this activity.

All of this could not have been accomplished without your
perseverance, creativity and industriousness. You are performing
a service not only for our students and our school but for the
entire community.

Also, I have enjoyed your description of our program in the recent
VEA Journal and would hope that others will emulate the things we
have been doing here at Bryant.

Thank you for your interest in helping to make the Bryant Retail
Work Program grow and grow and grow.

Sincerely,

Martin Ilivicky
Principal

MI:AB

News Articles

LONG ISLAND PRESS, MONDAY, DECEMBER 27, 1976   ☒ 5

A store is their classroom

By PETER BORN

For most Long Islanders, the euphoria of Christmas morning is by now the dread of bills to pay.

But for about 200 students in the retailing program at William Cullen Bryant High School in Long Island City, the holiday hangover means hassling with disgruntled gift receivers; looking for a better fit or more livable color.

The students — mostly seniors from working class families—learn the A B, Cs of employment from behind cash registers in shops, restaurants and banks up and down Steinway Street, as well as in Manhattan. Teacher Marvin Findling had started scouring up jobs for his students as the most relevant way to teach the often dull subject. The lessons brought more than knowledge.

The students grossed nearly $500,000 from their part-time jobs in a 12-month period, ending last June. Members of the Steinway Street Merchants Association were so upset by talk of budget cuts threatening the program, that the president, Julian Wager, wrote a letter urging Principal Martin Ilivicky to make sure it survives.

* * *

"FINDLING MOTIVATES these kids in a way I have not seen in a long time," Wager said. "We've gotten kids (as employes) who show an honest desire to learn and help out, unlike some of their counterparts. They're interested in earning for themselves and not taking."

And learn they do. When Sandra Forbes, 17, stands behind the counter of diamond rings and other expensive jewelry at Consumers Distributing in Forest Hills, her petite figure, long blond curls, and soft complexion conceal the heart of a pro.

"The 10 per cent discount always works," she said, revealing some tricks of the trade. "It's a small amount of money, but the customers go crazy. All of a sudden, they've got to have it today."

For those who are nearly hooked but retreat into "I'll wait until tomorrow," there is the "last chance close-out."

"I say: Did you know a lady just said the same thing about that ring, and I'm afraid it won't be here when you come back," the girl explained. "And I always let them hold it in their hand while they're deciding."

* * *

LENA TENAGLIA, also 17 of Jackson Heights, doesn't sell. She constitutes a one-girl personnel department at Citibank headquarters at 5th Avenue and 37th Street in Manhattan. Earning $3.77 an hour, she feeds information into a computer, so headquarters can keep up with the hirings, firings and retirements at 13 branch banks.

Banking, however, is not in her future.

She plans to open her own beauty parlor, once through hair styling school.

"I like to use my creativity, I want a real profession," said the girl who startles schoolmates by alighting from a taxi on cold mornings.

"There's a lot to learn here that you will use your whole life," said Tom Ferris, 17, of Woodside. He is another Citibank employe who earns $3.20 an hour and works 17 hours a week. His wages will help soften the blow of college tuition next year, but he sees greater rewards in his work studies. "Algebra won't do a bricklayer any good. We learn how to deal with people."

Reinaldo Perez, 18, of Astoria, has been selling clothes at the Boys and Mens Shop, 30-80 Steinway St., for more than a year. He draws $2.75 an hour after school and on Saturdays.

"It feels good to have responsibility," he said, adding that he particularly likes the independences of "not having to depend on my parents for money."

Asked what he would do with a customer wavering between two sets of jeans and the door, Perez quickly said he's made up the customer's mind for him. "Some ask my opinion, and I give it," he said. "Sometimes you have to push, but sometimes you don't."

But would he let a near-sale just walk out? "Oh no, I know better than that," Perez said with a laugh.

Retail Work Program Grows; Students Gain Credit, Jobs

Mr. Findling supervises the Retail Work Program, some of whose participants are meeting with him, above. Left to right: Sharon O'Dea, Paula Spatafora, Lisa Atkins, Carlos Blanco.

By Susan Behrens

"It's the hottest elective around." So says Marvin Findling, speaking of the Bryant Retail Work Program. Although created only two years ago, the program now has twice as many students enrolled in it as any other high school in New York City.

Mr. Findling, co-ordinator of the RWP, sees the enthusiasm growing. He cites one reason for the program's popularity as being the practicality of the class. "A lot of what students learn in school will never be used outside the classroom. The Retail Work Program is preparing them for life. The kids can feel this."

One RWP student, Annette Nardiello, agrees with this. "The class makes you more aware of yourself. It gives you confidence and teaches you how to work with people."

The success of the program has

and seven of his students demonstrated the skills learned in class at a meeting at the Board of Education November 25. Officials from the Cooperative Education Bureau, high schools, and colleges observed the students dramatize sales presentations and selling techniques. The school has been invited back in the near future. "Bryant's RWP has an excellent reputation," explained Mr. Findling.

The Retail Work Program is for students who wish to obtain part-time jobs after school in the field of retailing. A four-term retail work sequence is available. The sequence begins with Retail Work Preparation, continues to Retail Work Experience, Retail Products Information I, and then Information II.

Employers are asked to rate the students once a term for job performance, and this rating is

converted into a numerical grade worth one credit. This credit then becomes part of the students' school records. One credit is also given for passing the RWP class.

Because the demand for the class is so high, Mr. Findling must reject many students who would like to take the course. When a student applies, his academic, attendance, and lateness records are all taken into consideration.

The student learns about applying for a job, sales presentations, and related topics. Then a job is found for him. However, before a student is assigned that job, the "employability" of the student is checked. Forms are sent to all of his teachers asking their opinion in the matter.

Robert Meyer, Chairman of the accounting and distributive education department, estimates that there are 200 students now in part-time jobs because of this program. Taken together, these jobs bring in an income of a quarter of a million dollars a year.

Students of the Retail Work Program in Action

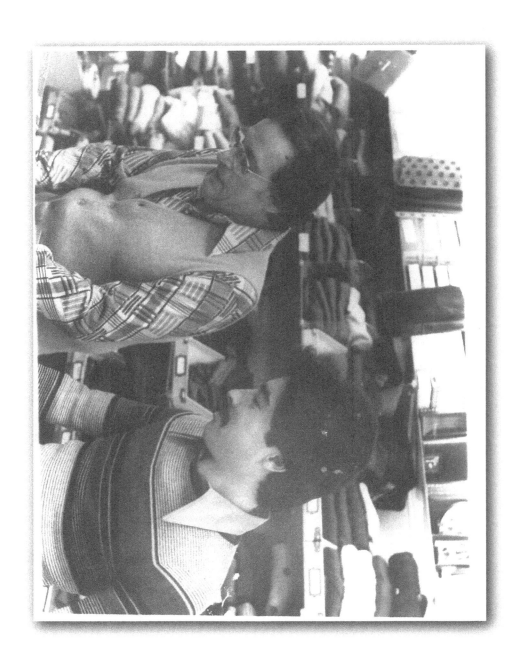

Other Schools

It was my good fortune to be permanently appointed to Bryant High, the **best** of the best.

Prior to the above, I had many experiences during my ventures through the school system, but the following were among the standouts.

Benson's Philosophy – Not Popular

The principal of the school, Mr. Joseph Benson, was not very popular with either students or faculty. His philosophy was to reign supreme, establishing his own rules and regulations, many in violation of the teachers' union contract. This included assigning faculty, including myself, to teach subjects that we were not licensed to teach, which was protested vigorously during faculty meetings.

Although there were many rebels opposed to his cause, he adamantly focused his retribution on a select few. His specialty was unannounced classroom visits, where he would find the slightest reason to give the teacher an unsatisfactory rating. This would become part of the latter's permanent record. For example, a teacher of earth science had a dental problem and a lisp that affected his ability to pronounce the word pith—as in pith ball—properly, this being the sole reason he was given an unsatisfactory rating following Mr. Benson's surprise visit to his classroom.

As the school's union delegate, I disputed the rating at an arbitration hearing. The final ruling was in the teacher's favor, and the unsatisfactory rating was removed from his permanent record. This really pithed off Mr. Benson

On Holy Thursday, Mr. Benson observed a class with only five students present. He found nothing wrong with the lesson, but he humiliated the teacher in front of the students by stating, "You wear that suit so many times that if you were home sick, the suit would come to work by itself."

On another occasion, he accused Melvin Miller, a teacher who was proctoring a Regents chemistry exam, of helping a student answer a multiple-choice question.

"I heard the student say, 'Mr. Miller, would it help if you got a better look?' And Mr. Miller, you actually pointed to the answer," said Mr. Benson.

I subsequently questioned the student regarding the incident.

She told me, "I knew I was in trouble in this exam, realizing that every little bit could help. I asked Mr. Miller if he could clarify a question on the exam. He stated that he really couldn't help me. Since I was wearing a halter, I leaned forward, offering Mr. Miller a better peek at my boobs, and asked, 'Would it help if you got a better look?' Mr. Miller pointed a finger at the four possible answers and said, 'It's either A, B, C, or D.'"

My position as the teacher's union representative who constantly opposed Mr. Benson's vengeful tactics against various members of the faculty had a very negative effect in our relationship. So it was no surprise that I eventually became his primary target. One day, during the Regents week, Mr. Benson heard a rumor that many teachers, myself included, had left school grounds between proctoring assignments—contrary to regulations—to have lunch at a local Chinese restaurant.

This was his moment.

Leaving school grounds without permission was a cause for suspension. He kept announcing over the school loudspeaker that I was wanted in his office. My not responding only increased his excitement, to the point where his secretary, Margie O'Brian, never really fond of him, told me that he sounded like he was experiencing an emotional orgasm. She called the restaurant and spoke to a teacher.

Margie said, "Tell all the teachers, especially Mr. Findling, to get back to the school as soon as possible, or face the same consequences that await Marvin."

Actually, I was never in the restaurant. I was in a school phone booth, placing a stock trade with Stocker, my broker, and didn't hear the announcement. Suddenly, someone was kicking the door of the phone booth. I looked up, and there was Mr. Benson, his face purple with rage, pushing, kicking, and almost succeeding in opening the door to the phone booth. I kicked back and did succeed in keeping the door closed. In doing so, I may have caused some damage to a couple of Mr. Benson's fingers.

He bellowed, "I want to see you in my office immediately!"

I stated, "I will be there, but first I have to go to the bathroom to take a pith."

My visit to his office lasted about one minute. He jumped up and shouted, "Were you out of the building today?"

"Nein, Herr Benson."

"Then you're dismissed. Our discussion is over."

"Danke, Mein Führer."

On the first day of school following the summer recess, it was announced over the school loudspeaker that Mr. Benson had passed away during the summer. The school shook with roars of approval from the students and teachers.

This was followed by equally resounding boos when it was announced that it was not Mr. Benson but his wife who had passed away.

Mad Myrtle

While relaxing in the teachers' lounge one Friday morning, I was approached by Ms. Myrtle Mudgett, one of the teachers in the English Department. She appeared to be distraught and almost on the verge of tears. Upon my inquiry about being so upset, Myrtle told me, "At the request of Mr. Goldman, the school principal, I appeared at his office yesterday. Mr. Goldman showed me an unsigned note that he found in his letter box, stating, 'At least 75 percent of the students in Ms. Mudgett's fifth-period English composition class have come to the conclusion that she is crazy and belongs in a loony bin."

Myrtle continued, "After allowing me to read the note, Mr. Goldmam said, 'Myrtle, there are times when your peers think your actions weird, considering the fact that you have been known to wear at least three dresses at the same time and appear to be growing a moustache. I have also heard that on occasion, you sniff snuff in the teachers lounge. At other times, you chew tobacco and then expectorate in a rather reckless manner, many times missing your spittoon. Nevertheless, Myrtle, I am in total disagreement with the composer of this letter.' Mr. Wilson's final comment did not assuage my upset feelings."

She went on, "When my class assembled today, I immediately passed out a slip of paper to every student. I then placed my bowler hat on top of my desk, at the same time demanding a confession from either the student who had reported me to the principal, or a witness to the perpetrator's actions. Otherwise, I warned, the entire class would face the consequences, including extra projects. After walking around the classroom and collecting the slips of paper in the hat, I commenced to read them aloud. Among the responses, or confessions, were the following, and I quote:

'It was Sir Isaac Newton's son, Fig.'

'It was me.'

'It wasn't me.'

'It was Joe DiMaggio.'

'It was my Aunt Tilly.'

'It was John's other wife.'

'It was Babe Ruth.'

'It was Malcolm X.'

'It was Sherlock Holmes.'

'It was John Lennon.'

'It was me, and I'm glad. Glad, do you hear? Glad!'

'I love you, Myrtle. Will you be my turtle?'

'It was Benito Mussolini's girlfriend, Tootsie.'

'If my grandmother had balls, she'd be you'

'It was the Shah of Iran.'

'It was Adolf Hitler.'

This entire experience has left me very upset."

After hearing her story, I stated how much I empathized with her, and then I proceeded to ask, "But Myrtle, why do you wear so many dresses at the same time?"

Her reply: "It's none of your fuckin' business."

Untrue Confessions (Lies)

On the second day of the school year, I was approached by Robert Miller who, because of his youth, good looks, and personality, was one of the most popular teachers in our school, especially with the female population.

Robert asked if l could help in resolving a rather delicate situation. Apparently, during the past summer, Robert was a guest at a Club Med resort. He became enamored with a young lady named Stacey. Robert told Stacey that following his graduation from law school, he was offered and accepted a position with the Federal Bureau of Investigation. His latest assignment was to track down a counterfeiter who was passing off hundred-dollar bills and was believed to be a guest at the resort.

Stacey then told Robert that she was an undercover police officer, assigned to the resort under the guise of being a young college student. She would be attempting to gain the confidence of another guest, traveling incognito, who was a major supplier of various narcotics, including cocaine and heroin. He was especially known to seek out teenagers, ply them with drugs, and then exploit them for his own devious purposes.

Robert and Stacey agreed to combine their individual missions into a joint venture, and for practically the entire week, they would lounge at the pool and smoke pot. They were waiting to be approached by the figments of their imaginations, with Stacey being enticed with drugs, and Robert catching the culprit in the act of passing out counterfeit hundred-dollar bills.

Each evening they would have dinner, revisit the lounge, dance, and smoke more pot, while still awaiting the arrival of their suspects. They would eventually retire for the evening, but not before rewarding each other with the comfort of finding a release for the emotional strain that was the result of pursuing their laborious daylong activities.

Although the daily negative results of their imagined joint venture were somewhat disappointing, Robert and Stacey agreed that the fringe benefits made for a great week, and they parted with promises to get together in the future.

Well, getting together happened much sooner than anticipated.

On the first day of school, who should be sitting in Robert's history class, but none other than Hilda Schwartz—alias Stacey.

The situation was resolved. As a follow up to my conversion with Robert, Hilda/Stacey paid a visit to her guidance counselor, where she expressed her enthusiasm for the field of law. I was subsequently approached by the guidance counselor and gave permission for Hilda/Stacey to be transferred from Robert's history class to my criminal law class.

Stacey was an excellent student and received ninety-plus as her final grade.

Following graduation, she attended the John Jay School of Criminal Justice and became an officer with the NYPD, eventually becoming involved in undercover activities.

Isn't truth stranger than fiction?

About the Author

Marvin Findling earned his Bachelor's of Business Administration from Baruch College, New York, and completed his educational courses at Fordham and New York University before going on to receive a Master's of Educational Administration and Supervision from Pace University. He is a charter member of Phi Delta Kappa.

Prior to his teaching career, Mr. Findling gained his retailing knowledge as a sales manager for The Fuller Brush Co., the same company the Reverend Billy Graham sold products for on a door-to-door basis, and credits for his additional perseverance in delivering his sermons.

Mr. Findling is currently a senior financial representative for the Northwestern Mutual Life Insurance Co.